The Complete Book of

Retro Crafts

The Complete Book of
Retro Crafts

Collecting, Displaying & Making Crafts of the Past

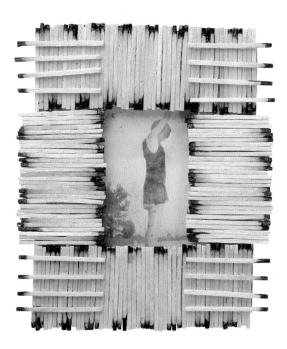

Suzie Millions

LARK BOOKS

A Division of Sterling Publishing Co., Inc.
New York / London

Editor
Ronni Lundy

Art Director
Suzie Millions

Cover Designer
Cindy LaBreacht

Illustrators
Jennifer Jessee
Suzie Millions
Lance Wille

Photographer
Steve Mann

Library of Congress Cataloging-in-Publication Data

Millions, Suzie, 1958-
  The complete book of retro crafts : collecting, displaying & making crafts
of the past / Suzie Millions.
      p. cm.
   Includes index.
   ISBN-13: 978-1-57990-869-0
   ISBN-10: 1-57990-869-1
   1. Handicraft. 2. Arts, American--20th century. I. Title.
   TT157.M495 2008
   745.5--dc22

                                            2007022797

10 9 8 7 6 5 4 3 2

Published by Lark Books, A Division of
Sterling Publishing Co., Inc.
387 Park Avenue South, New York, N.Y. 10016

Distributed in Canada by Sterling Publishing,
c/o Canadian Manda Group, 165 Dufferin Street
Toronto, Ontario, Canada M6K 3H6

Distributed in the United Kingdom by GMC Distribution Services,
Castle Place, 166 High Street, Lewes, East Sussex, England BN7 1XU

Distributed in Australia by Capricorn Link (Australia) Pty Ltd.,
P.O. Box 704, Windsor, NSW 2756 Australia

If you have questions or comments about this book, please contact:

Lark Books
67 Broadway
Asheville, NC 28801
(828) 253-0467

Manufactured in China

ISBN 13: 978-1-57990-869-0

For information about custom editions, special sales, premium and corporate purchases, please contact Sterling Special Sales Department at 800-805-5489 or specialsales@sterlingpub.com.

To my mother, Louise, my son, Andy, and my husband Lance, listed in descending order relative to the number of years they've had to put up with me.

Contents

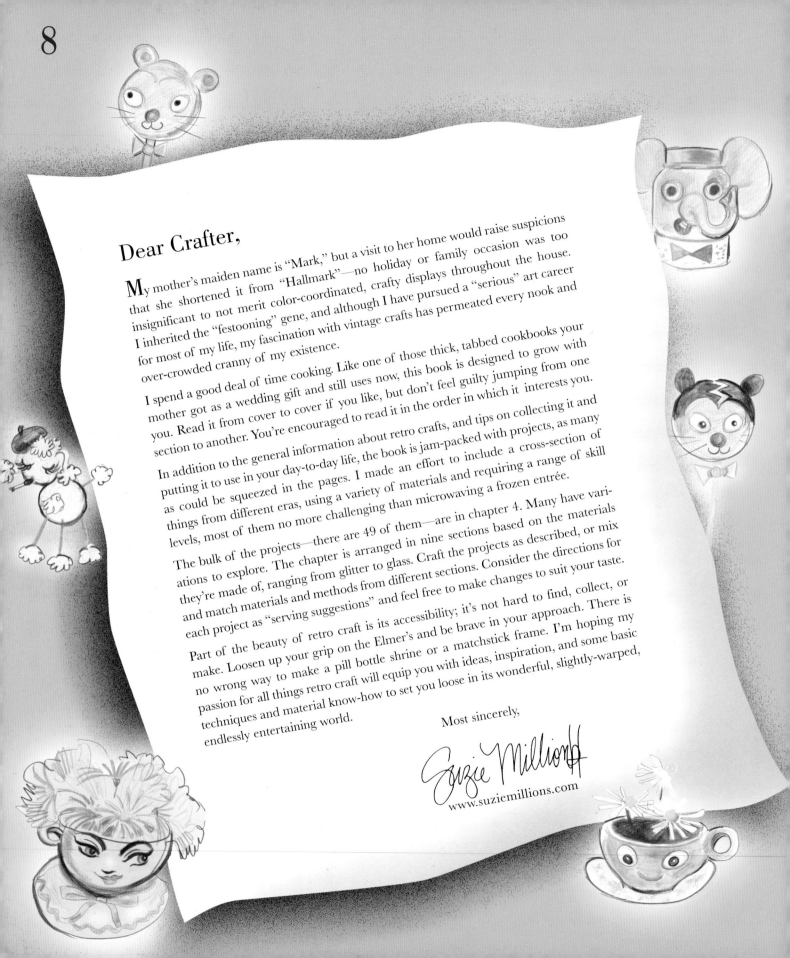

Dear Crafter,

My mother's maiden name is "Mark," but a visit to her home would raise suspicions that she shortened it from "Hallmark"—no holiday or family occasion was too insignificant to not merit color-coordinated, crafty displays throughout the house. I inherited the "festooning" gene, and although I have pursued a "serious" art career for most of my life, my fascination with vintage crafts has permeated every nook and over-crowded cranny of my existence.

I spend a good deal of time cooking. Like one of those thick, tabbed cookbooks your mother got as a wedding gift and still uses now, this book is designed to grow with you. Read it from cover to cover if you like, but don't feel guilty jumping from one section to another. You're encouraged to read it in the order in which it interests you.

In addition to the general information about retro crafts, and tips on collecting it and putting it to use in your day-to-day life, the book is jam-packed with projects, as many as could be squeezed in the pages. I made an effort to include a cross-section of things from different eras, using a variety of materials and requiring a range of skill levels, most of them no more challenging than microwaving a frozen entrée.

The bulk of the projects—there are 49 of them—are in chapter 4. Many have variations to explore. The chapter is arranged in nine sections based on the materials they're made of, ranging from glitter to glass. Craft the projects as described, or mix and match materials and methods from different sections. Consider the directions for each project as "serving suggestions" and feel free to make changes to suit your taste.

Part of the beauty of retro craft is its accessibility; it's not hard to find, collect, or make. Loosen up your grip on the Elmer's and be brave in your approach. There is no wrong way to make a pill bottle shrine or a matchstick frame. I'm hoping my passion for all things retro craft will equip you with ideas, inspiration, and some basic techniques and material know-how to set you loose in its wonderful, slightly-warped, endlessly entertaining world.

Most sincerely,

Suzie Millions

www.suziemillions.com

List of Projects

There are 9 fun and fabulous sections of retro craft here to amaze and amuse you. If you have trouble deciding where to start, spin a pen cap on the page and start with whichever project the end of it points to...

* Indicates Quick as a Wink projects

Chapter 1

What is
Retro Craft?

OF A DIFFERENT ERA
HANDMADE
HEARTFELT

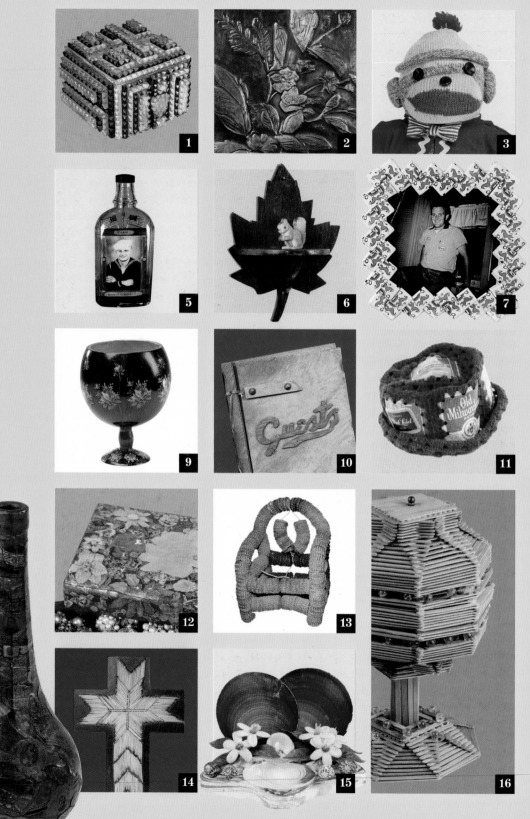

Say what?

Here's a visual aid to help put some faces to the names:

1. Tramp art box
2. Copperplate relief
3. Sock monkey
4. Postage-stamp collage
5. Whimsey bottle
6. Knickknack shelf
7. Paper chain frame
8. Paint by number
9. Coconut goblet
10. Scrapbook
11. Beer can hat
12. Decoupage box
13. Bottlecap toy chair
14. Matchstick cross
15. Shellcraft ring dish
16. Popsicle stick lamp
17. Cigar band vase

Howard Gosnell whimsey bottle (no. 5 above): Courtesy Michael Williams Collection

Opposite, from top: **Campers tooling copper reliefs**

Bottom: **Paper chain box,** Dorito bags, 12 x 6 x 4 inches

I Don't Know What It Is, but I Made It Myself

The Good, the Bad & the Really Ugly

Calypso-themed bottlecap men, folded paper chain picture frames, matchstick crosses, and glitter-encrusted pine cone elves: these are retro crafts. So are fuzzy pom-pom rabbits, angels made from folded *Reader's Digest* magazines, and southern belles adorned in gowns of plastic beads and safety pins. The retro crafts in this book span the five decades from the 1920s through the 1960s.

The term craft is a big umbrella. When defining retro crafts, think of that umbrella as being made of bendy straws and paper doilies.

These handmade treasures were often made with simple materials and household scraps. They required little skill or training. Anybody could, and almost everybody did, make them.

High crafts, exquisite objects labored over with great skill and dedication, are not retro crafts, regardless of the era in which they were made or the materials. Part of what makes them different is that high crafts were created by accomplished artisans with a developed aesthetic, an aesthetic influenced by natural ability, professional training, or generational tradition.

Grandma may have taught you how to make a knitted beer can hat, but that hat is decidedly retro craft. There is a low-brow aspect at work here. That's part of its charm. It's direct and unaffected. In the vast and ever-more elite and sophisticated art-world buffet, retro craft is the warm and familiar Toll House cookie.

Everybody's Doing It

Crafts were thought of as art for Everyman. In this country, for almost a century, hardly a fifth grader graduated to the sixth without having been introduced to some form of craft or another. Elementary school, Scouts, Sunday school, vacation bible school, summer camp, and 4-H were all craft-churning fun factories. And that's only counting the kids. Crafts were routinely included in rehabilitation programs for people recovering from injury, illness, and emotional stress, even those being rehabilitated from antisocial behavior. (At least we hoped they were being rehabilitated and not just fashioning their craft supplies into googly-eyed weapons.) Beyond the incapacitated and incarcerated, there were legions of adults who made crafts for fun, fulfillment, and/or profit. These voluntary and involuntary crafters left behind mountains of retro craft. You, too, may have contributed to this massive and diverse body of work.

Some of these works are hobby crafts assembled from kits or published directions, others

Googly-eyed guy with a gun
Wood, pipe cleaner, duct tape
3½ inches tall

are mutants inspired by the popular craft of their day, while still others are unique products of personal vision, assembled from household castoffs, and varying degrees of imagination and spare time. The worst pieces collect dust at the thrift store, the ugliest little puppies at the pound. The best of retro craft blurs the lines dividing art and craft, crossing into the realm of folk art.

Flip toy
Wood, plastic doll, paint
10½ inches tall

Wishing You Were Here

Outside the Box

A mid-1960s vacation stop my family made to visit the formal gardens and gift shop at the prison in Marquette, Michigan, also revealed a whole lot of crafting going on. I remember velvet paintings, pictures made from feathers, and a bevy of naked ladies tooled into leather belts and pocket books. When I asked my mother years later why we visited the prison, the story got even stranger—she thought I was asking about the time we went to the state prison in Jackson, Michigan. Turns out the family interest in prisons and their gift shops stemmed from my grandfather's love and pursuit of velvet paintings. (My interest in all things low-brow would appear to be hereditary.) Never thought of my folks as outside the box thinkers, but their choosing penal institutions as vacation destinations proves me wrong.

Craft kit with yarn
1962
Included everything but the yap for transforming bottles into fuzzy pink poodles

Missing Links

There isn't a crisp border between recognized folk art and retro craft, and there are pieces that straddle that fuzzy border with a foot on each side. Like missing links in archaeology, these pieces help demonstrate the connection between the two worlds.

I regard the two objects on this page—a naive but passionate wood carving of a bird and a small lamp fashioned from cast-offs—as missing links. Neither has could-stake-your-life-on-it artistic worth, but both have a nagging sincerity and personal vision that make them hard to dismiss. Both pieces demonstrate ingenuity with limited materials. You can almost feel the artists' smugness about using what was at hand. It's hard to tell whether or not they were made following printed instructions. Either could have been the product of a shop class. They both appear to be hand-rendered by someone who was artistically untrained. I like these two particular examples because, as you observe the similarities between them, you are forced to pay closer attention to and recognize the validity of the more-difficult-to-embrace piece, the lamp.

The mellow tone of the wood, the simplicity of the shapes, and the subtle colors used by the bird carver give that piece an elegance that makes its artistic merit evident. At first glance, the gum wrapper and plastic spool lamp is easy to dismiss as a bunch of junk, which it is. But someone cleverly and patiently took materials that most of us would toss in the trash and fashioned something both ridiculous and sublime out of them. This lamp almost screams, "Down with the commodity culture!" And on closer examination, its subtle artistic merits are revealed. I like that the gum wrappers work as color-fields. I like the unintentional way the paper that wasn't covered with tape darkened. I like the way that dirt settling on the edges of the tape makes a frenzy of lines, like county boundaries on a state map. If the lamp's maker had just needed some extra light around the house, he could have stopped at the first spool, but it's tiered and tapered, like a skyscraper, with a wonderful bolt-columned plaza below.

As time passes, the materials used to make it will become less familiar, transforming the lamp into a time capsule and the lamp maker into a conveyor of historical information.

Learning to take a closer look at what you might reflexively dismiss is a good exercise for expanding your thinking before entering the world of retro craft. It may help you to actually see retro craft pieces around you that you might otherwise overlook. It may also help you to approach materials, both traditional and non-traditional, more creatively when making retro craft.

Lamp
Plastic spools, gum wrappers, transparent tape, bolts
9 inches tall (base)

Bird carving
Wood, paint, glass
9 x 10 inches

Retro Craft on a Pedestal

Movin' on Up

Heated scholarly debate over the definition and boundaries of folk art—outsider, brut, visionary, et al—has been going on so long, it no longer qualifies as "raging." It's more a persistent smolder. Regardless of which camp of art geeks wins the arm wrestle on that one, folk art will probably remain the weird uncle at the art family reunion, with its unruly kin retro craft not likely to receive an invitation to the picnic any time soon.

In the summer of 2004, Chicago's Intuit: The Center for Intuitive and Outsider Art, featured an inspiring hobby craft show, *Outside the Lines: Ordinary Pastimes, Extraordinary Art*. The show included hundreds of items representing dozens of types of retro craft loaned from private collections. The co-curator of the show, William Swislow, authored an informative and generously illustrated article, "Common Crafts, Uncommon Art", printed in Intuit's *Outsider* magazine (Volume 8, Issue 3, Spring 2004, pages 21–29). The show and the article were a rare and encouraging art-world acknowledgement that a connection between retro craft and folk art does exist.

Interior, Intuit Gallery

Top of page:
WWI Victory Banner
Buttons and mixed media
35 x 20 inches

Glass objects with matchsticks, gravel, cigar bands, torn paper, and colored sand

Classifying the Déclassé

In the article, Swislow got down to brass tacks defining retro craft. He identified 80 things as "forms of self-expression most available to the artistically untaught." This is to retro craft what the periodic table of elements is to science. Many of the items listed have extensive subcategories, but I'm hard-pressed to think of a form of retro craft he has not classified. For your convenience, his work has been abbreviated on the handy shopping reminder at right. You can read the full list at interestingideas.com/out/craftshow/craftside.htm.

Lamp
Wood, Popsicle sticks, marbles
19 inches tall
Shade, 12 x 12 inches

Left:
Matchstick sphinx
Matchsticks and mixed media
25 inches tall

RETRO CRAFT
Shopping Reminder

- Beaded Objects
- beer Can hats
- BirdhOuses
- Bottlecap constructions
- Ceramics
- Christmas decor
- Cigar band collage
- Coconut art
- Copperplate relief
- cutout lawn ornaments
- Decorated Hangers
- Decorated Pillows
- Decoupage
- driftwood SCulpture
- Embroidery
- Folded wrappers
- Greeting card Baskets
- Hair Pictures
- Homemade clothing
- Hooked Rugs

- Horseshoe Sculpture
- Jewelry
- Junk Sculpture
- Knick knack shelves
- Knitting
- Macaroni art
- Macrame
- Make do (pincushions, etc.)
- Matchstick Constructions
- Memory objects
- NeedlePoint
- Nut Sculptures
- Paint By Numbers
- Painted Saws
- Pop top constructions
- Popsicle art
- Postage stamp collage
- Pot Holders
- Quilts
- Root sculptures

- Safety pin structures
- scrapbooks
- Seed art
- Shell art
- silent Butler
- Sock Monkeys
- Spin Art
- Spool furniture
- Spoon ARt
- String aRt
- Tin can furniture
- toothpick constructions
- Tramp Art
- Trench Art
- twig Furniture
- Watch Part pictures
- Whimsey Bottles
- WhiTtling
- wood burning
- Woven Baskets

William Swislow serves on the board at Intuit and is a frequent contributor to the Folk Art Society of America's magazine, *The Folk Art Messenger.*

Crafting at Grandma's house

What Is the Significance?

Valuing the Intangible

Retro crafts have obvious nostalgic value. They often pull at heartstrings, calling up thoughts of family and childhood. There are probably traumatic crafting memories out there, but for most of us, retro craft kindles recollections of lazy afternoons, milk and cookies, Grandma's house, and simpler times.

Retro crafts are a part of our pop culture. Like Crayola crayons and *Gilligan's Island*, they connect many of us with one another. All retro crafts evoke an era, from the spartan, utilitarian objects of the 1930s, born of the forced ingenuity of hard times; to the irreverent, glittery, outer-space-inspired pieces from the 1950s, to the earthy, brown-paletted fiber constructions of the eco-conscious late 1960s. When it comes to revealing their age, most retro crafts say it loud, say it proud.

Like a view through a dusty window, retro crafts offer intriguing hints about the people who made them. Non-kit crafts were often made from household scraps, and so reveal what average folks had lying around the house, or what was available at the local five and dime. Kit crafts, designed to be appealing and affordable to as wide an audience as possible, serve as a snapshot of middle-American lifestyles and aspirations. They're a time-frozen reflection of our culture, its fads, and trends.

Arranging a collection of crafts chronologically from the early 20th century to the present illuminates the gradual progression in content and form, from naive pieces revealing their forthright rural roots, to polished, sophisticated works that hardly even appear to be handmade. As our culture moved forward, craft marched right alongside it, pipe cleaner arms swinging.

Red bird
Cast plaster, paint
8½ inches tall

Retro craft fulfills a longing for things that are personal and handmade. There can be a homogenized sameness in the materials available at the giant craft chains of today: precut wooden shapes, premixed paints, faux gems and sequins in the most popular (but only the most popular) colors, fool-proof mix-and-match coordinated papers, mini die-cut and laminating machines. Modern crafts constructed entirely with these materials can suffer from a blandness that washes out the originality and warmth that were once the strong suits of handmade crafts. Yes, there are imaginative modern craft designs, but the sheer perfection that many of those projects require obscures the very sense that they were made by human hands. Part of the appeal of retro craft is that these things are not just handmade, they are often so very obviously handmade.

> "...these things are not just handmade, they are often so very obviously handmade."

Handmade does not necessarily imply artistic worth. There's plenty of bad retro craft out there, but ironically, some of the least interesting pieces are the ones that were executed with the highest degrees of skill and faithfulness to directions. Often the more interesting pieces are those that suggest the crafter, intentionally or not, strayed from the paved roadway and made a new path. The resulting piece conveys a sense of humanity and personal vision, no matter how humble or flawed.

Earth to Grandma

The ultimate retro craft anthem, *Earth to Grandma*, was penned by Chuck Cleaver of the Cleveland, Ohio, band, Ass Ponys. A line from the chorus says it all, "Earth to Grandma, What the hell is that?" Check out the song and complete lyrics on the 1994 A & M release, *Electric Rock Music*. It features a dazzling retro craft Christmas decoration on the cover.

Shell belle
Plastic doll, shells, foam ball, and trim
8 inches tall

Copperplate relief
Copper, plywood
8 x 6 inches

Note: The imagery on this piece is a retro craft Rorshach test. I see it as a car climbing the track on a roller coaster, but it has also been identified as a tank on a bridge, a rocket on a launch pad, and a toy on the banister of a staircase.

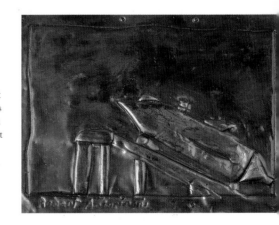

Top left:
Photo album
Wood, suede straps
10 x 13 inches

Less Can Be More

Some flawed pieces have slid down the slope of artistic worth so far that they enter the realm of absurdity, and there take on meaning in their utter ridiculousness. They insist that you consider how they came to be: What could that crafter have possibly been thinking? Some make you laugh, spontaneously and incongruously. There's a wooden plaque in my kitchen that has a simple rendering of a cardinal on a branch. The crafter cut the bird and branch from wood, mounted them on a couple of more layers of wood, carved in some details, and added some paint. Something is amiss, and when you sort that out you realize that the bird's eye is below his beak, where his chin would be, if birds had chins. That's only mildly odd, but even though I've owned it for years and see it all the time, that misplaced detail can catch my eye from across the room and make me laugh out loud.

Bird plaque
Wood, paint
9 x 9 inches

Beauty can be found in imperfection. Manufactured perfection encompasses everything these days, from the synthetic rock walls lining the highways to the caps on our teeth. Rather than enriching our senses, uniform perfection seems to dull our perceptions. Maybe that's why more and more people are seeking out objects that have the feel of something caringly made by a human being. Retro crafts were often labored over with sincerity and love. A matchstick box that was nothing more than a Cub Scout project accomplished in an afternoon was, nevertheless, for that afternoon the entire focus of an eight year old who loved his mom. Fifty years later and tattered, the box still emanates his heartfelt devotion and earnest desire to please.

Macaroni boot
Child's marching boot,
macaroni, gold paint

Church
Wood, linoleum
16 inches tall

Cub Scouts displaying projects
Photo courtesy Amos Craft Publishing,
Sidney, OH 45365 USA
From *Pack-o-Fun* magazine,
August–September, 1964

Imperfection
By the Number

Multiple examples of the same retro craft project made by different crafters illustrate the subtle, and in some cases not so subtle, qualities that make each piece distinctive. Nothing demonstrates this better than the same paint by number kit rendered by different people.

There are meticulous painters who painstakingly stay in the lines. These attention-to-detailers are prone to obsess about the paint texture too, keeping it as smooth and brushless as possible.

There are painters whose motto is "close enough," dabbing the colors in the approximate area where they were intended to go. Some of the close-enough painters also subscribe to "that's good enough," not bothering to repair drips or smears, eager to move on to the next bow-crested poodle or cloud-capped purple mountain.

Then there are the freestyle painters who, pre-printed canvas be damned, veer from the course and improvise with colors, experiment with blending, and sometimes even add their own embellishments to the subject matter. Their intention to improvise and the consistency with which they do distinguishes them from my favorite category of by-the-numbers painters, the truly challenged.

These artists, through bad eyesight, inattention to detail, or even dyslexia, complete and then proudly frame works with glaring errors. My favorite example is a portrait of Jesus in which the painter clearly muddled the highlights above Jesus' brow. Filling in what should have been light flesh with dark brown paint, the artist gives this Lamb of God the sweeping scowl of a Klingon warrior.

As your collection grows, you recognize that the paintings, like darts around a dartboard, circle the bull's-eye with varying degrees of accuracy. (Klingon Jesus would be an errant dart stuck in the wall.)

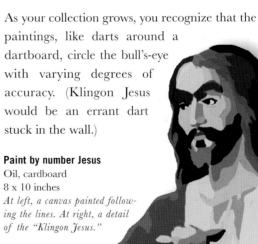

Paint by number Jesus
Oil, cardboard
8 x 10 inches
At left, a canvas painted following the lines. At right, a detail of the "Klingon Jesus."

Chapter 2

Retro Craft Preparedness

The Nitty Gritty on Work Space

1 Light

2 Work surface

You can dive right into making retro craft with nothing fancy required. All you need is light and a surface to work on. For generations, retro crafts have been put together under flickering fluorescent lights, on dinette sets, tiny school desks, and wobbly folding tables.

If you have an itching-to-make-something monkey on your back, feel free to skip right ahead to Projects. I'll even make it easy for you! The projects start on page 46.

But if you're interested in setting up a more serious work space or tweaking one you may already have, read on. The following chapter is all about how you can do just that.

Instant Craft Space Idea #1: Ironing Board & Clip Light
An ironing board is a quick, easy, uncluttered surface for light crafting. For extra work space, clamp a sheet of foam core under the clip light.

Instant Craft Space Idea #2: Picnic Blanket and Sunshine
Toss down a vintage tablecloth for the quickest, easiest craft space of all.

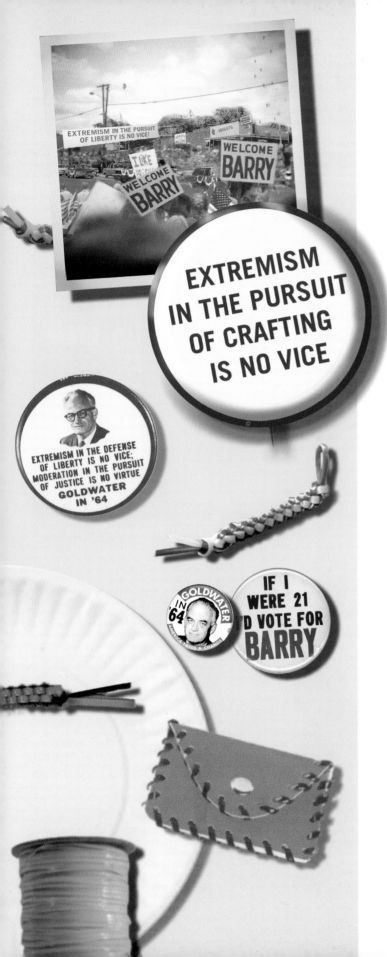

*Mementos from my earliest
craft camp days*

Stop & Think It Over

You may already be a card-carrying craft fanatic reading this from your immaculately appointed, pegboard-lined craft cave. Or you might be a first-time crafter who has never done a project but now finds the allure of transforming coffee bags into stylish folded chain frames simply irresistible. In either case, there are some things it would be helpful for you to know about the how, where, and what of an effective retro-craft work space, and I am the person with the trial and plenty of error lifetime experience to tell you.

One of my earliest crafting memories involves sitting at a craft camp picnic table making vinyl lanyards while watching Barry Goldwater's Presidential campaign procession drive by. It's been pretty much continual crafting ever since. Along the way I've gained some insights into what makes a functional retro-craft space.

My work space.

Labels in image:
- GPS SYSTEM
- HANGING WIRE BASKETS
- RAGS
- FINISHED PROJECTS FOR INSPIRATION
- THINGS I'M THINKING ABOUT USING
- GLITTER STATION
- PAPER PLATES FOR PALETTES
- EVEN MORE LIGHT
- LIGHT
- MORE LIGHT
- BOOKSHELF
- DESSERT SHELF
- GLUE GUN STATION
- FREQUENTLY USED TOOLS
- HANDY INDEX CARDS
- STORAGE
- CANISTER AND TRAY, FOR REFERENCE PROJECTS
- TOOTHPICKS
- PAINT WATER STATION
- OLD MARKER BOARD TOPPED WITH GLASS
- CUTTING MAT
- FLAT WORK SURFACE
- CLAMP
- YARDSTICK CUT TO FIT DESKTOP
- TOOLBOX (OOPS, YOU CAN'T SEE IT)
- FREQUENTLY USED SUPPLIES

Your Work Space

Essentials & Then Some

A retro-craft space isn't very different than any other craft space. The basics are a sturdy work surface, good lighting, and storage. Handy electrical access and a sink are a plus. A mini fridge and a record player with at least a thousand records would be a plus, plus, for me. You'll need to think about what makes a work space ideal for you. Here are some of the things you want to consider:

Are you about to have a fling with retro craft, or do you anticipate a lifelong affair? A temporary space set up for pre-Christmas projects can be much more flexible than the one you'll need if retro craft is about to become a fixture in your life.

Does the space need to be kid friendly?

Do you want natural light?

What level of creature comfort do you require?

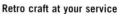

Retro craft at your service
A coffee carafe on an enameled tray on a squirrely knickknack shelf makes a handsome paint water station.

Once you define your wants and needs, compare them to the resources you have to work with:

What space is already available? If you have the option of working in a space separate from your living space, that's another decision you'll need to make.

What's the size of your budget?

At first glance, your needs and resources may seem to be worlds apart, but using the same sort of creative re-envisioning and make-do ingenuity that is the very spirit of retro craft, you may discover the perfect craft space right in your own backyard. Hey, what about a little trailer tucked under that pear tree? One of my favorite work spaces was a craft-equipped Airstream; then again, I've had just as much fun working on a tray table in my living room.

You may need to make trade-offs and maybe even sacrifices to find your space. It's a matter of setting priorities. For years, even in minuscule apartments, I made my kitchens serve double duty as studio space. I used kitchens because of the easy access to a sink and storage. My son grew up thinking nothing of bags of cement and mason jars full of aquarium gravel in the kitchen cupboards and pantry. Meanwhile, pots, pans, and baskets of baking supplies hung from hooks in the ceiling. (I used mosaic materials more often than I used the baking powder and brown sugar.) I always replaced bulky stoves and refrigerators with skinny apartment-size models and shoved them to one area, as much as their cords and the gas line would allow, making all the room I could for creative space. I was determined to have a dedicated work space set up and ready to go. My stock configuration included a sturdy table, a tea cart, and cheap metal shelves.

Just as I refigured the purpose of my kitchen, you may be able to adapt yours, or the laundry room, or an infrequently used extra bathroom, a walk-in closet, or a corner of the living room where nothing gathers that often except dust.

There are books devoted entirely to the topic of craft space, and scads of articles in magazines and on the web. Reading them can give you nuts and bolts specifics and inspiration for how to adapt someone else's idea to make it work just for you. And that's the bottom line: do what works for you.

> "...using the same sort of creative re-envisioning and make-do ingenuity that is the very spirit of retro craft, you may discover the perfect craft space right in your own backyard."

Crafty workshops
You can turn an old shed into an artistic work space. A vintage trailer that isn't roadworthy can still be craftworthy.

Dedicated to the One I Love

A dedicated craft space is a room, a nook, a cranny, or any space in which your tools and materials, fixtures and supplies can stay put. A couple of advantages to this sort of space are:

The Waltz In, Waltz Out: Everything is set up and ready to go. You don't have to waste precious craft-making time dragging boxes and carts out of the closet or out from under the bed, or tracking down tools from this corner and that. If you don't live alone, having your tools and supplies segregated from daily household use (possibly off-limits as well) can minimize frustration. The easier it is to get started, the more productive you're likely to be.

Commitment: Taking the time and effort to set aside space for crafting is a pledge to yourself that you'll return to it sometime and make wonderful things.

Like a piece of exercise equipment in your home, it's a gentle reminder that you've decided to make this part of your life.

Focus: Having a designated craft space helps keep you focused while working. Even if that space is just a corner of a room, when you step into that corner, it's with a purpose. Being surrounded by art-making supplies, projects in progress, and things that inspire you is creative rocket fuel.

Fun: No getting around it, having your own personal, dedicated craft space is fun. Appointed with things you love, it's an extension of your creativity. When friends and family visit, bring them in to play Show and Tell with your latest projects.

Initially, being able to leave a mess (unfinished projects and supplies scattered about) seems like another advantage to having a dedicated craft space. But my experience has taught me that it actually defeats the benefit of The Waltz In, Waltz Out. If the bits and pieces of a project-in-progress are splayed out all over your workplace and you want or need to work on something else, you first have to sort through the clutter and debris to find tools and supplies, and then you'll have to work around the mess. It's easy to lose track of things for your current project amidst the stragglers from the projects past, not to mention losing momentum and focus in the disarray.

Nothing Fancy *My junk store appointed work space suits me just fine. Hand-me-down cabinets, picnic baskets, and old suitcases provide flexible storage. Presto-chango, instant shelving was made from discarded windows and heavy glass, supported by dresser drawers and glass blocks.*

Your Tools & Those "Extra Something" Somethings

The Toolbox

Before you start your first project, get yourself a tackle box or toolbox (in a size slightly bigger than you think you will need) for organizing smaller tools and some frequently used supplies. The specific tools and supplies you need will depend on the projects you work on, but check the list at right for the basics.

I like to keep a few creature comforts in my toolbox, including a tiny sewing kit, pain reliever, and candy. If there's something you don't function well without, and it will fit in your toolbox, toss that in too. My toolbox includes ponytail holders, a pair of generic emergency earrings, and red lipstick.

More Tools

Additional essential tools that are nice to have in your workspace include:

   24" metal straightedge
   Craft saw
   Miter box
   Motorized craft tool
   Assorted screwdrivers and clamps
   Measuring tape
   Drill

Be absolutely methodical about designating specific places to keep each tool and returning them to their specified places after each use. Always.

Toolbox Basics

Craft knife and spare blades
Metal straightedge (as large as will fit in your box)
Very sharp paper scissors
Large scissors (for cutting items other than paper)
Pinking shears (or your favorite paper edgers)
Hole punches
Brushes (bristle and foam, in several sizes)
Glass cutter
Small hammer
Snub-nose pliers (with a wire cutter)
Small roll of wire (18 gauge or so)
Tape—electrical, packing, and transparent
Mini glue gun & glue sticks
Small tube of white glue
Decoupage medium
Thumbtacks
Paper clips
Pencil & sharpener
Permanent marker
Assorted gel pens
Tubes of glitter
Very small cutting mat
Extension cord

Additional Appointments

Project Shelves

Instead of stashing projects-in-progress and projects-in-the-planning-stages in a closet, box, or storage tub, consider equipping your work space with open shelves designated just for projects. Keeping projects out in the open keeps them not-out-of-sight, not-out-of-mind. That helps keep the momentum going. I find I often get inspiration for one project while working on another. Repeatedly walking by and working near them helps make that possible. I think sometimes my brain works on things subconsciously while I'm occupied with something else. Keeping the shelves project-specific and not cluttered with other things provides a clarity that makes the not-out-of-sight aspect more productive, and makes it easier to gleefully choose what project you want to move on to the next time you get that precious craft time. Use shelves that fit your style and your space.

When you leave your work space, put unfinished projects onto trays, into cardboard "flats," box lids, or whole boxes if needed, and slip them onto your project shelves. If you have supplies that are specifically for that project, put those in there too; otherwise, put them back where they came from.

In addition to works into progress, keep the elements for projects you're planning, but haven't started yet, on your project shelves. As you find materials and supplies for that project, drop them into the appropriate tray or box.

Limbo Shelf

One of my project shelves is devoted to materials that I'd like to use but don't know for what. Items currently languishing on the Limbo Shelf include a Piggle Wiggle game board from the 1940s, a blue velvet souvenir pillow, a stack of Perry Mason novels featuring some especially handsome dust jackets, four copper brackets (found with plumbing supplies) that will make perfect hairpin legs for a box, a jar full of burned-out lightbulbs, a jar full of flash cubes from the 1960s (I find them at yard sales), and a stack of hand-embroidered doilies.

The Versatile Box Lid & Grocery Flat

Cardboard box lids and grocery flats make great storage trays for projects-in-progress, projects-in-the-planning-stages, and all kinds of crafting materials. The lids to the boxes for reams of paper are ideal. Copy and print shops are a good source, and most are generous about letting them go.

Grocery stores, dollar stores, and convenience stores receive lots of things in cardboard flats and simply throw the flats away after stocking the shelves. You can make your request to recycle their trash easier to accommodate if you find out when the shelves are stocked and come by to pick up the emptied flats then.

Project shelves
Trays, baskets, and cardboard flats hold projects in progress. The board on the bottom is the Limbo Shelf.

Jerry Lee Lewis & the Theory of Creative Rocket Fuel

Years ago, I had a magical experience at the legendary Hernando's Hideaway, a smoky, cavernous, old barn of a club in Memphis, Tennessee. Sitting at a table maybe 15 feet from the stage, I heard confident fingers glide across the keyboard. I looked up in astonishment to see the house band surrendering the stage to Jerry Lee Lewis. As I watched him play with a ferocity that was exceptional even by his standards, I couldn't help but notice that he was transfixed on a single point at the front of the stage. Curious, I worked my way through the crowd to discover that the focus of his attention was a whole-lot-of-woman in not-so-much-denim, shake-baby-shaking-it just in front of him. For nearly two hours without pause, she distressed her denim, while he played the keyboard like he was trying to pound it through the floor.

That night I developed my Theory of Creative Rocket Fuel: Whatever our level of talent—minuscule, immense, or in between—there are some things that not only seem to have the combination to our creative locker, but also amplify our natural abilities. And, like running a hot wheels car through a super charger, or packing a big woman into little jeans and putting her in front of Jerry Lee, they can make what is great even greater. Learn to recognize the things that spur you creatively, and keep them in your work space.

Project Shelf Favorites

Suzie Do

Old bakery racks

with big industrial wheels and large, removable metal trays make dynamite project shelves. The wheels make them easy to move around, and the removable trays make the shelf height adjustable. It's convenient to store a project on a tray, pull it out and work on it while it's still on the tray, and then slide it back into the rack when you're finished. Chain grocery stores often have old equipment warehouses that sell used bakery racks at very reasonable prices. They can also be found in junk stores and metal scrap yards. If money isn't an issue, you can purchase one new from a restaurant equipment source or industrial supply catalog.

For a quick, cheap, and simple project shelf, commandeer an old stepladder. Rickety is okay. A ladder that's too wobbly to stand on can still work fine as shelves. Moving from the bottom of the ladder to the top, slide progressively shorter-as-you-go boards on each step. It may amaze you how much can be accommodated in a limited amount of space. ✳

Inspiration Shelf

Find a visible and accessible place to display things that inspire you. Actual retro craft objects and pictures of retro craft are good sources of inspiration, but include other things that have colors, shapes, and textures that spark your imagination. I have a bunch of inspiration shelves throughout my house and studio. The one I wouldn't want to live without is an old hutch situated directly across from my bed so I see it every night before I fall asleep and every morning before I get up. It holds postcards from the early 20th century, a tin chicken coop and plastic chickens, a taffy box with retro graphics, pinecone men, a miniature stone grotto from Germany, a small stenciled sign left behind after Mardi Gras, souvenir items encrusted with rocks and shells, a round cage from an old bingo game filled with marbles, a picture of my son taken one memorable summer day when an unanticipated train breakdown led to an afternoon of adventure and discovery in Mississippi, and lots of other unrelated things that in some way spur me creatively.

Idea Box

Whenever inspiration hits me, I jot down ideas on index cards. (Sometimes the idea is purely my own, and sometimes, when I'm browsing through a magazine, a shop, or online, it's someone else's idea that I want to borrow.) Folios for carrying loose index cards and spiral bound card notebooks are easy to find, and I carry one with me always.

Later, I file the cards in my Idea Box, a small plastic recipe file I keep in my work space, where it's handy to flip through when I need a creative nudge.

The Idea Box has dividers for different kinds of projects. There's also a section labeled "Seeds of Ideas" where I file ideas about using imagery or materials when I'm not sure what type of project to use it for, and a section labeled "Supplies" where I file information about supplies and vendors, including labels from packages and website addresses. When I see materials or tools that I might like to use eventually, but don't need at the moment, I record the details of what it is and where I can find it, including contact information from the package, if that's available. If it's in one of those cavernous home centers, I record the aisle number, too.

The Idea Box is also a great place to keep notes about projects you've worked on. You may have a breakthrough about what to do, what not to do, or an inspiration for a different approach you might want to take in the future. (I love trying new approaches, and I especially love avoiding making the same mistakes twice.) Put those things down on cards and file them under the project headings so that next time you work on that type of project, you'll find them. Like the hand-scrawled notes in your Grandma's cookbook, those insights can be invaluable.

Start maintaining an Idea Box. I bet you'll be amazed to see how many ideas you have. When your box gets too full, that just means you need to start making things.

Idea Box dividers and cards
Make ridiculously crafty dividers out of sized felt (the stiff stuff).

Why All the Fuss?

After revealing all the fussy, compulsive things I do to equip and organize my studio, it might seem like a massive gear change when I say, "Now relax and just wing it." But having a well-appointed, well-organized space paves the way for care free crafting. Trying to be creative without forethought and organization is akin to trying to put together a meal in a dirty kitchen. Unless you have an affinity for calamity, getting yourself set up beforehand makes retro crafting much easier and so much more fun.

Put things that inspire you to use in your work space!

A pipe cleaner character nested in a flocked plastic candleholder holds a favorite pair of scissors and brush at the ready. Napkin holders, plastic card trays, a ceramic planter, and a toy airport all pitch in to bring order and levity to my desktop.

Idea Box

Tray prepped for making Animal Pals Party Picks (page 165)
Gathering components and setting them out neatly on a tidy tray make it fun and easy to think projects through and put them together.

Montessori Method

1 Preparation

2 Execution

3 Cleanup

Ever envy those cooking show chefs who slide out a tray filled with small bowls containing all the necessary ingredients, chopped, sliced, diced, and ready to go, and who have every kitchen tool and appliance needed at arm's reach? They may not call it this, but those chefs are using the Montessori Method. A visit I made to a Montessori school years ago taught me this very practical approach to tasks. Every task consists of three parts: preparation, execution, and cleanup. Until then, I had struggled to keep organized; this philosophy was life changing for me.

It has helped me with everything from cooking to laundry to crafting, especially crafting. And it can help you.

Going into a project fully anticipating and budgeting time for the preparation and cleanup, as well as work time, makes for more peaceful, less harried creative time. And having all your prepped tools and materials at your fingertips is nothing shy of the star treatment. Try applying the Montessori method to your crafting.

Chapter 3

Make Like a Squirrel

The Nitty Gritty on Supplies

Each project in chapter 4 has a list of the materials you'll need for making it. If you want to dive right into making some without further ado, let your fingers do the running straight to page 46.

But if you feel the urge to dig a little deeper first, continue reading here for some clever ideas for reusing old things and remaking new things to stock your supply shelves.

Era Appropriate Color & More

Unsure what colors, patterns, textures or overall style choices are accurate for the era? A ladies' magazine from the same time period is all that you need. Look at the cars, clothing, and home decor.

Note the package designs for cosmetics and groceries featured in the ads, and the designs of the ads themselves. Note the typefaces and decorative elements used. Graphic designers set and reflect trends, and their work is a distillation of the popular culture of their time

Pay special attention to how colors were used together. Mimicking not only the colors, but also the way they're combined is a subtle but really effective way of making things look like they're from a particular time.

Big seasonal department store catalogs are also great references. Many items were offered in a choice of colors, sometimes illuminated by tidy insets showing the palette.

Early 1950s' muted and tertiary color palette

Look beyond the obvious. There are lots of color and design choices from every era. If you're working in the 1950s, for instance, don't settle for pink and turquoise. There are scads of other cool combinations. Trends come and go, and what was once all the rage can be all but forgotten later. Finding something less obvious may take a little more digging, but will give your work that extra twinkle.

Old School

Boxes So Pretty You Can't Bear to Open Them

Vintage craft supplies are still out there, showing up in thrift stores and yard sales. I love coming across them. The packaging is usually dreamy. If it's super-dreamy, I just hang them up somewhere as inspiration. Some supplies, such as glitter and sequins, come in odd colors that are hard to find now. I consider them "Special Reserve" and set them aside for the perfect project. Of course, you don't need actual vintage craft supplies to make retro crafts. You just need to find materials that have the look and feel of the era you want to convey.

Scrap-o-Rama

Judging from the fruits of their labors, old-school crafters took delight in rethinking, reusing, and recycling just about everything within reach. On close, and sometimes not so close, examination, much of their handiwork reveals an ingenious use of ordinary household discards, including scrap lumber, glass jars, fabric, buttons and other sewing notions, matches, Popsicle sticks, postcards, thumbtacks, greeting cards, wrapping paper, cardboard, cans, and bottle caps, to name just a few. Lots of these things haven't changed that much over the years and can be used with little or no alteration. There are also many simple ways you can make new things look old, as the following sidebar, Aging Sleight of Hand, explains.

Left:
Bottlecap person
10½ inches tall
This scrappy Cappy features margarine tub bowls, pop bottlecap arms and legs, a hatpin nose, screw eye ears, and festive curtain ring earrings
Above:
Colorful vintage clothespins

Hoarding 101

Stock your retro-craft supply shelves with cast-off items from your household. Some usable and versatile hoardables include:

- *Bottles and jars*
- *Bottlecaps and jar lids, metal and plastic*
- *Plastic bread bags with retro graphics*
- *Cans with printing directly on the can (foreign grocery items are a good source of these)*
- *Interesting can labels (remove them and store them with your vintage papers)*
- *Aluminum beverage cans (cut off the neck ring and store rolled together; see page 75)*
- *Coffee bags*

Clean things up and let them dry thoroughly. Store them in designated containers.

I keep big, pretty old jars and baskets in my kitchen to collect my hoardables. I leave them out in the open so it's easy to drop things in when I take them out of the drainer. The interesting containers help make the collections seem more like part of the decor and less like part of the clutter. (My craft space is not in my house, so when the kitchen containers fill up, I empty them into plastic bags and file the contents with the other supplies in my space.)

Aging Sleight of Hand

A few tricks can make brand new look like retro

Darkening: Make a batch of strong tea. Find a container that will hold the paper covered with the tea, but make sure it's something that you won't miss for a day or two. A metal or plastic letter tray, sauce pan, or cake pan will work. Put the paper in the container and cover it with The Death Tea. The amount of time you leave it in depends on the type of paper you're using and the type of effect you're going for. Frequently, overnight does the trick for me.

Paper

Fading: Bright sun will fade most papers and commercial inks. A sunny windowsill will work, or try the always brutal back window of your car. In a hurry? Get creative at the copy store; experiment with different settings on the color copier. Lay a sheer, gauzy fabric, waxed paper, or very sheer tracing paper over the glass, and color copy your image from behind it.

Wearing: Bend! Fold! Spindle! Mutilate! Play a little rough with paper to give it some instant age. Roll up the corners and rub the paper against itself. Crease, wad, and then flatten it out again. Lay it facedown on a sidewalk or driveway, and walk on it. Put the paper on the seat of your car, and drive around with it under you. (I was just having fun with you on the car seat bit, but now that I think about it, I wouldn't rule it out.)

Etc.

Bucket-O-Rust: This one is extremely high tech. It's also a great way to age metal and, surprisingly, several other materials. Put the stuff you want to age in a can or bucket, cover it with water, and leave it. I'm not a scientist, but it seems to work faster when I use a metal bucket. Rust—it's not just for metal anymore. It will settle on other things, too. It works especially well on white buttons with thread still in them.

Amber Varnish: Decorative artists working for the House of Blues in New Orleans taught me that anything you want to add age, depth, and a sense of warmth to will benefit from a coat or two of amber varnish. It's readily available in most home centers and hardware stores. Too bad it doesn't work on lame pseudo-blues bands.

Amber Varnish

MIRROR
ROSETTES

HAIRPIN CLIP

CAP NUT

LOCKING
WASHER

SCREW CAP

CAP HEX NUT

RUBBER
STOPPERS

Shopping for Faux Retro

Shopping for Specifics

Despite dedicated hoarding and adroit use of scraps, there are times when you're just going to have to break down and buy stuff. When you're shopping for materials for a specific project, don't be too shy to bring along reference material: a vintage book, pamphlet, or magazine, or an actual craft piece of the time or photograph of one. Choosing materials with textures or colors that closely mimic the ones used in the era makes a big difference. Bringing in a reference may also help

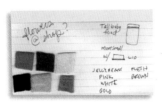

Felt samples glued to an index card make a handy color reference to bring along when shopping.

the sales clerk better understand what you're looking for. You might find some clerks who enjoy the originality of what you're doing and become eager collaborators in helping you find what you need.

The Hardware Stroll

Hardware and home stores are slap silly full of things to use in retro craft. Every now and again, I do a little thing I call The Hardware Stroll. I start at one end of the store and walk up and down every single aisle. Every single aisle. Don't skip even one.

Somewhere near the screws and bolts in most large home centers, there are cabinets full of amazing little odd things you never knew existed, just crying to enter the world of retro craft. Take time to look carefully through the drawers, and to imagine how you might be able to use these gizmos.

So many interesting, affordable things in the hardware store can be used for something other than their

Using Something for Something Else

Disconnect your rational brain and throw out assumptions when shopping for retro-craft supplies. Plug in on your imagination to see new uses for familiar stuff. Clear round furniture floor guides make cheap, interesting frames. The little white X-shaped spacers used between glass blocks make excellent ornamental doodads. A cake-decorating tip can be an elegant penholder.

I try not to abuse the privilege of free paint chips, but very occasionally, if I need just a speck of paper in a special color and can't find it, I "contemplate" changing the color of my dining room, if you catch my drift. (If you've been to my house, you know I don't have a dining room.)

intended purpose. Copper pipe fittings from the plumbing aisle make great legs for a box, or bases for plastic foam heads (see the Bottle Buddies on page 114). If you need small pieces of metal trim to use for the railing on a crescent moon shelf, or to decorate the edges of a frame, you can find them and other curiously shaped metal pieces with the furnace supplies. Cut roofing shingles or vinyl floor tiles to make great tops for Matchbox Drawers (page 125).

The Stroll also works for supply shopping in one of those Everything-Is-Ridiculously-Cheap stores, art and craft supply stores, and even the grocery store. If you're lucky enough to come across a Mom-and-Pop hardware store, take time to explore it. They're great places to find quirky things, sometimes things that aren't even made anymore.

Supplies can be stashed in canisters, secondhand food storage containers, vintage tins, and not-so-stylish but cheap and handy cardboard boxes. Flimsy hair processing caps from a beauty supply store work really well for covering buckets, boxes, and smaller containers to keep dust and critters out.

Organizing Supplies

The Art of Containment

Most of my supplies are in cabinets and on shelves in my work space. Some I keep in baskets, hanging from the ceiling. I use lots of plastic bags to help keep things sorted but still easy to view.

Everything-Is-Ridiculously-Cheap stores are a great source for a variety of storage containers from food keepers to buckets to large plastic bins. The clear bins are ideal so you can see what's inside at a glance. But the opaque ones are sometimes less expensive and will work well if they're labeled clearly.

Storing Things So You Can Find Them

Because so many supplies are used in a broad range of projects, I organize them based on the type of material, not by what I think I'm going to make them into. To find something, all I have to do is ask myself, "What's it made of?"

Your categories may be different, but the ones that work for me, and a sampling of the things they include are listed here.

Glass	*Sheets of glass as well as items made from glass (ashtrays, plates, bottles, marbles)*
Metal	*Flat sheets, hairpins, bottlecaps, cans*
Wood	*Popsicle sticks, toothpicks, matchsticks, shaped woodcuts, small lumber scraps*
Naturals	*Stone, pinecones, shells*
Paper	*New paper, vintage papers (scraps from magazines, books, greeting cards, wrapping paper, paper doilies), tissue paper, transparent mylar, cardboard and heavy stock (including old and new boxes), book board, game boards*
Plastic	*Vintage bakery picks, toys of all sorts, plastic bottle caps, colorful straws, and stirrers*
Sewing	*(My only exception to the "What's it made of" concept. These items are classified according to their original use.) Buttons, rickrack, lace, fabric scraps, felt, thread, yarn*

In each category, I separate new-from-the-store items from found objects. When I'm designing projects, it's helpful to know what I can easily run out to buy more of, as opposed to what may take years of rummaging to replace.

Retro Imagery

The Real Deal

Using vintage imagery is a simple way to make your craft project seem as if it's out of the past.

Family photos are something most of us have access to. Use them generically to convey a particular era, or use them to customize very special family gifts. For instant ancestry, use someone else's family photos. It's sad to see them discarded, but photo albums, snapshots, and framed portraits are easy to find in the junk world. (The great images in all the Glitter Frames on pages 52 and 53 came in frames purchased at a junk store.)

When junking, keep your eyes open for vintage books and magazines. Cookbooks, dictionaries, children's encyclopedias, and storybooks are retro imagery goldmines. Old postcards and record album covers provide glossy images on a heavy surface. Things you may not normally think to look for, but that can be great sources of retro imagery, include old wrapping paper, greeting cards, yearbooks, catalogs, maps, can labels, and all kinds of ephemera. Old scrapbooks are often packed full of "all of the above."

Make scans or color copies when you want to preserve the original source. I keep most of my vintage imagery in large storage tubs, with a separate Special Imagery notebook for things I consider exceptional.

ZINNIA

This recently discovered family photo is in my Special Imagery file, on tap to be used soon. The cakes were part of an April birthday celebration. My mother's cakes were always special, but this particular bunny cake is burned in my memory, having caught fire on the way to the dining room table! The flames from the birthday candles ignited the paper ears and then took off like a brush fire through the dried coconut.

Special Imagery File

Keep a notebook filled with clear plastic sleeves for images you're especially eager to use. The sleeves help protect what can be very fragile pages, making it easy to browse through the imagery without causing any wear and tear. I like flipping through my file, as if I'm shopping from a catalog. My file includes a few favorite photographs, some vintage postcards and nice old greeting cards, the cover from a Gene Autry comic book I intend to make into something for my mom, and a couple of clippings from mid-century magazines.

I also have an "oversize" file that I crafted from poster board. (A paper art school portfolio would work, too.) The oversize file includes several full pages from vintage magazines, and an especially nice print of cacti.

Be selective about what you put in this Special Imagery file. You want it to stay lean. If it gets bloated, the really special things will get buried in the clutter.

Presto Retro

If you don't have the time, inclination, or resistance-to-dust to be an ephemera hunter, there are some very good clip art publishers that offer vintage imagery online and in books. The images won't be unique since they're so widely available, but they're easy to use and less messy and musty than originals can be. Pseudo retro imagery—modern imagery made to look vintage—is out there too, but I roll my googly eyes at most of it because it tends to be cheesy.

Chapter 4

Roll Up Your Sleeves
& Fetch the Glue Gun

Cardboard — paint by numbers, cereal/grocery boxes, game boards, flattened soda can, record album covers, puzzle box lid, playing cards, greeting cards

Imagery — books, comics, pulp novel covers, everything on the first wheel, photographs, color copies of fabric, wrapping paper, candy wrappers, can labels, magazines

Rods — pick-up sticks/tinker toys, sticks (the barky kind), wooden dowels, insulation supports, bbq skewers, pencils, bamboo, copper pipe

Swaparama

For easy material swaps, try to think of other materials that could work in the same way as the material you are planning to use.

Substitutions, Please!

The projects are arranged by the principal materials used to make them, but don't let these categories confine you—experiment, mix and match, bring your own ideas.

The ideas for substitutions offered in the *Swaparama* illustration above are provided as a bit of grease to get the mental gears working. Could something made from stiff cardboard be made from metal instead? Foam board? Tile? Glass? Could something put together with tape be made using tacks or eyelets, or could it be stitched together with yarn? Leather or vinyl cord? Can you use a can, a cup, or a cardboard box as a starting point, instead of building something from scratch?

Sometimes I make a substitution using materials that are around the house instead of buying something, and sometimes I substitute just for the fun of making something more my own.

Another reason to substitute is to tweak projects to fit the occasion at hand. A chart showing suggestions for occasion specific variations is on page 172.

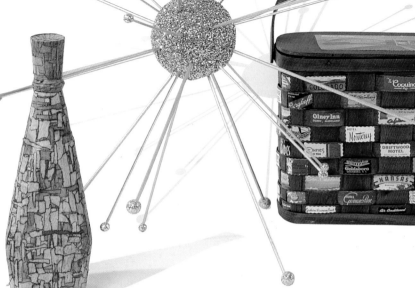

Craftacular!

A Smorgasbord of Choice

In the 1960s, when my midwestern family wanted to indulge in shameless consumer choice, we loaded into the station wagon and headed straight to the local smorgasbord. I can still recall the excitement I felt when I settled my tray on the rail. Greeted first by a jiggling spectrum of gelatin cubes, the rail led to an ice-field of crispy green salads, a regimented army of steaming, sturdy white china loaded with meats and vegetables, and last, a whipped-cream-capped wonderland of pies, cakes, puddings, and cobblers. Memories of the soggy, overcooked food have faded; what I remember is the dizzying parade of choice.

Grab your tray and sidle up. The projects in this book were selected to give you that same blissful feeling of seemingly endless choice. They represent a diverse mix of things made with all kinds of materials. When special tools could be helpful, they're mentioned, but none of the projects here require costly equipment or advanced skills. Materials used are easily found and affordable; a lot of them are scraps and household castoffs.

Some projects are very simple—a Cub Scout with the attention span of a flea could do them. Others may require you to put down the cocktail and read the directions carefully.

Time to Have Fun

Clear your head space; lighten up. Remember that these projects were born in a less exacting time, a pre-double-mocha-torte era when mom could wow the bake sale with a cake made from a box and decorated with gum drops and mini marshmallows.

Gather the tools and materials you need. Assemble some inspiration. Get into your comfort zone— a retro comfort zone. Pop a Perry Mason episode in the DVD. Put on a vintage apron. Take breaks for milk and cookies. Have a blast.

Ladies and gentlemen, plug in your glue guns!

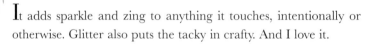

All That Glitters

It adds sparkle and zing to anything it touches, intentionally or otherwise. Glitter also puts the tacky in crafty. And I love it.

So did the Victorians (and we all know the legacy of taste and restraint in decor that they left behind). The first examples of glitter crafting I can find are embellished postcards from the Victorian era that were turned into wonderful Christmas ornaments by adding even more glitter and tinsel cord. Double dipping.

I'm Melting, I'm Melting

Vintage glitters were made from metal foil, making them chunkier and more reflective than a lot of the flimsier plastic film glitters you see now. Modern plastic glitters are also prone to melt. Often it's hard to tell what you're getting, since some glitter bottles are labeled "aluminum and/or plastic." You'll know for sure what you're working with when you shake some into a bit of hot glue and it dissolves into an iridescent puddle. Anything made with petroleum products, including glues, spray paint, varnishes, and some sealants, can also melt plastic glitter, or strip it of its reflectivity and iridescence.

Good old-fashioned white glue or decoupage glues are always safe, and there are water-based sealers you can use. If you're in doubt, make a test patch on a piece of paper, and experiment before you try it on your project. Sometimes it takes a few minutes for the product to strip the glitter, so wait a bit before assuming everything is okey dokey.

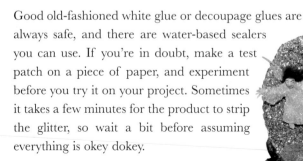

Glitter in Moderation

Outside the Box

It's easy to go from zero to 60 with glitter. Experiment with using it sparingly. A line around the edge of something, a sprinkling of tiny polka dots, or other precise accents can provide just enough flash without the trash.

Paint vs. Glue

Expect glitter-encrusted objects to shed. Even when coated with sealer, glitter tends to flake off. Instead of glue, use acrylic paint as the adhesive, in a color similar to that of the glitter. With the paint underneath, missing flakes of glitter will be missed a little less.

The paint must be very wet when you shake on the glitter. Over large areas, paint and glitter in sections until the object is covered.

For even better sticking power, you can mix white glue with paint, about half and half. The mixture will take longer to dry, but the glitter does seem to hold. If you're making a quick place card, don't bother with the blend; but for a keepsake object, take the extra time and trouble.

Note that the paint-as-adherent method doesn't work well with plastic foam. You'll need to paint the foam first, allow the paint to dry, and then use glue to adhere the glitter.

Sealing your sparkly thing will help keep the glitter on it. After the glitter has thoroughly dried, coat it with a clear sealant that you've determined to be safe. Either brush or spray on will work.

Hello Trouble

Now a rare word of practicality from me: Glittering a high-use object is asking for trouble—sparkly, gets-all-over-everything trouble. Glitter is best used on decorative, not functional, items. (Refrigerator handle, bad choice; rowing machine, good choice.) Keep this in mind before you get glitter happy. (My son might be quick to point out that I glittered the vinyl roof on my 1969 Ford LTD. Despite high speeds and inclement weather, it's actually held up quite well.)

The Glitter Station

A favorite comedian, Demetri Martin, aptly describes glitter as "the herpes of craft supplies." Confining it while you're working with it will keep it from becoming a part of everything you make. A good way to do that is to use a glitter station, a shallow cardboard tray or box lid and a stack of paper. Lay a piece of the paper in the bottom of the tray, hold whatever you're glittering over it, and shake, shake, shake on the glitter.

Still holding the item over the glitter station, give it a good shake to remove any excess.

Pick up the paper and curl it slightly to funnel the glitter back into its container.

Use a fresh piece of paper each time you use a different glitter in the glitter station.

If you apply more than one glitter to something, patience, Grasshopper. Let one glitter dry completely before adding the next.

Cardboard

Glitter Frame

Materials

Template A on page 53 copied onto cardstock
Two 5" x 7" pieces of cardboard
Glitter
Fine gravel *(pictured: aquarium gravel in a neutral shade)*
Tacky craft glue
Picture *(approximately 3½" x 4½")*
Glue dots *(optional)*
3" x 4" piece of clear plastic *(optional)*
Hot glue
Old CDs or small squares and bits of mirror, shells,
    sequins, and/or pennies for decoration
Self-adhesive picture hanger

Tools

Craft knife
Straightedge
Pencil
Box lid large enough to hold the frame
Medium brush for glue
Hot glue gun
Crummy scissors

Vintage glitter frames are often decorated with pieces of blue mirror. Blue glass is easier to find. Slip a little piece of mirror behind the blue glass to get the same effect. I like cutting pieces from CDs because they're easy to work with, and I always have plenty of them rolling around under the floor mat of my car.

Prepare the base

1 Cut out the template with the craft knife and straightedge, first the inside window, and then around the outside edges.

2 Trace the template on both pieces of cardboard.

3 Cut around the outside edges on both pieces of cardboard, but only cut out the inside window opening on one. The one with the window is the frame front, and the other is the back.

4 Mix equal parts of glitter and gravel in the box lid.

5 Brush a substantial coat of tacky craft glue on the frame front. Put it facedown in the box lid, and press down evenly. Lift it up and shake off the excess.

6 Position the picture in place on the frame back. Lay the frame front over it to make sure the picture is properly aligned. Glue the photo down using the glue dots or a light coat of craft glue around the outside edges. If you're going to put clear plastic over it, do that now.

7 With the picture facing up, run a bead of hot glue around the outside edge of the frame back. With the glitter side of the frame front facing up, press it down onto the frame back, lining up the edges. Press and hold for a minute until the two pieces are bonded firmly on all edges.

Have at it

8 Decorate the front of the frame. If you wait till the glitter and gravel dry, you can use glue dots to adhere everything. If not, use the tacky craft glue. Use the crummy scissors to cut small squares and slivers out of the CDs. They crack a little on the surface, but I like the way that looks. Wheat-back pennies or other old coins make the frame look vintage.

9 Glue the picture hanger to the center of the back.

variation
Horseshoe Glitter Frame

This lucky horseshoe frame is put together just like the basic glitter frame. Tinted CDs, paper flowers, and aqua sequins lining the entire edge give this one a little more color. Bottlecaps were flattened with a hammer and cut in half with tin snips to trim the inner frame.

Templates
Copy at 350% to make as pictured

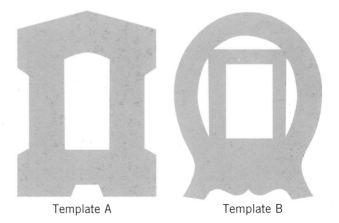

Template A   Template B

Sparkling
Sputnik

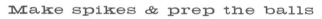

Materials

Acrylic paint *(same color as glitter)*
27 bamboo skewers
26 small plastic foam balls
Hot glue
1 larger plastic foam ball for base
Glitter
White glue
Masking tape
2" long piece of 20-gauge wire
Pretty cord

Tools

Shop rag
Metal skewer, awl, or other sharp, pointy object
Hot glue gun
The Glitter Station (page 51)
Brush for acrylic paint
Bowl large enough to accommodate the large foam ball
Brush for glue
Paper cup *(or something to hold white glue)*
Marker

Bamboo skewers work perfectly for this project. They're just the right length, sharp on the end so they're easy to get into the foam, and they're cheap! They vary in thickness, but all seem to work well. Use wooden dowels if you're making a really big sputnik. Paint with nail polish or cover in glitter glue instead of ordinary paint to make the skewers sparkly. As a step saver, use berry sprays from the floral section of the craft store for the small balls. They come in clusters of a dozen or so in a variety of sparkly, glossy, and metallic finishes. They have a soft, foam core, but the outer finish is usually a little crusty. Use the metal skewer, awl, or sharp, pointy object to poke holes for the bamboo skewers. *

Suzie Do

Make spikes & prep the balls

1 Fold the rag a couple of times to make a thick pad, and pour a little paint on it. Rub it on all but one of the bamboo skewers to coat them in color. (It's easy to get splinters, so be sure the rag is thick.)

2 Poke a painted skewer into each small ball. One at a time, pull out each skewer, put a drop of hot glue in the hole, and push the skewer back in. These are your spikes.

If you're using pre-glittered balls, go directly to step 9.

3 Poke the unpainted skewer into the big foam ball. Use it to hold the large ball so you can paint and glitter it without your fingers becoming a gooey mess.

4 Paint the big foam ball first and then the smaller ones.

5 Set up your glitter station so it's nearby and ready to go. (After the next step you're going to have to fly into glitter mode lickety-split.) Pour the glitter into the bowl.

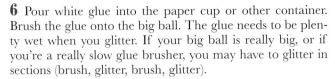

6 Pour white glue into the paper cup or other container. Brush the glue onto the big ball. The glue needs to be plenty wet when you glitter. If your big ball is really big, or if you're a really slow glue brusher, you may have to glitter in sections (brush, glitter, brush, glitter).

7 Working in the glitter station, hold the big ball by the skewer and roll it in the bowl of glitter, scooping the glitter on to cover any bare spots. Shake off the excess. Set aside.

8 If the small balls need to be glittered, glue and glitter them one at a time. Set aside to dry along with the big ball. (It could take hours. Have a three-course snack. Phone a chatty friend. Make a tiny, festive village out of your unpaid bills.)

Assemble the majestic orb

9 Take the naked skewer out of the big foam ball. Insert the first four spikes. Envision a clock and place them at 12, 3, 6, and 9 o'clock. It may make inserting them easier if you poke a guide hole first using the metal skewer. The more precisely you place the first four spikes, the more evenly the rest of the spike placement will go. I like to put a little piece of masking tape on these first four spikes and label them "1, 2, 3, and 4." It keeps me from getting confused during the assembly process.

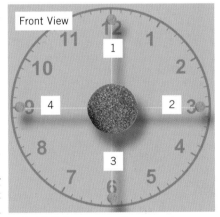

10 Add two more spikes with spike five evenly centered between the first four spikes, and at a 90° angle to them (see inset) and the next spike in the same position on the opposite side.

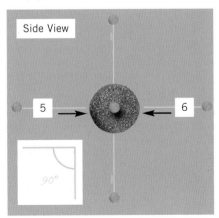

11 Add eight more spikes, with four in front and four in back as shown in the illustration.

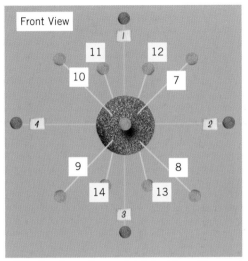

Spikes 7 to 10 are placed on the front of the sputnik, while spikes 11 to 14 (labeled with the gray boxes) are placed on the back. This is the basic sputnik configuration. Sometimes you may want to stop spiking here. For the super-spiky silver one on the opposite page, continue on.

(The first four spikes are labeled with masking tape)

12 Add four spikes between the initial four, following the red arrows on the illustration at right.

13 Add the last eight spikes, four in front and four in back, following the white arrows on the illustration at right.

14 One at a time, pull out a spike, put a drop of hot glue in the hole, and reinsert. Hold until firmly set.

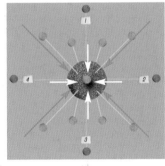

Slap a hanger on this puppy

15 Bend the wire into a U shape, and insert it deep into the top of one of the small balls at the end of a spike. Pull it out, drop a little hot glue in the hole, and put the wire back in. Take the tape off the first four spikes.

16 Tie the cord onto the U-shaped wire, and hang.

variation

Beauty Orb

Materials

3" plastic foam ball
Stem from a disposable glass
Hot glue
2" round mirror
Glitter
White glue
13 plastic hair roller pins
Glass-head straight pins and sequins *(oh so optional)*

Tools

Steak knife or craft saw
Metal skewer, awl, or other sharp, pointy object
Hot glue gun
The Glitter Station (page 51)
Bowl, large enough to accommodate the foam ball
Paper cup or something to hold white glue
Medium brush for glue
Rag

1 Use the steak knife or craft saw to shave a slice slightly wider than the 2" mirror from the foam ball.

2 With the cut side of the foam ball turned to the side, use the skewer or sharp object to poke a hole in the bottom of the ball. Push the plastic stem into the foam 1" deep.

3 Pull the stem out, put a big puddle of hot glue in the hole, and push the stem back in, holding until it's firm.

4 Put a circle of hot glue on the back of the mirror, and press it onto the shaved spot on the ball.

5 Set up the glitter station. Put the glitter in the bowl. Pour white glue into the cup.

6 Holding it by the stem, brush the ball with white glue. Roll it around in the bowl of glitter, scooping and sprinkling glitter to cover. Shake off the excess. Wipe any mess off the mirror.

7 Place the hair roller pins following steps 9 to 11 for the Sputnik, with the exception of the one pin obstructed by the mirror (first half of step 10). For extra beauty, skewer sequins or beads on glass-head straight pins, and stick them in willy-nilly until you are awed.

Apply Sputnik Technology to all kinds of things

Dress up a buffet table: Cut a large plastic foam ball in half, wrap it with foil, and stick it to a plate with a dollop of peanut butter. Spike it with skewers full of shrimp, cheese, vegetables, or anything tasty you can stick on a skewer. A dessert sputnik sounds yummy to me, bejeweled with chocolates, glistening cherries, and donut holes.

Entice a toddler: Instead of skewers, cut colorful drinking straws in half and serve up fruit balls, cheese, cubes of bread, hot dog slices, and other diminutive delectables.

Make a desk model: Add a mirror and base, and the Sputnik becomes a Beauty Orb. The one pictured uses a disposable Margarita glass stem for the base. Other ideas for bases include shampoo or other plastic bottle caps, copper couplings from the plumbing department, the stem of a cheap plastic goblet (snip it off with garden pruners), or use an old-school meat thermometer.

Make your bar exemplary: Wrap small plastic foam balls in foil and drop into martini glasses. Spike them with colored toothpicks. Top each with olives, cherries, or cocktail onions. For extra flash, use a tiny disco ball (sold with accessories at the auto parts store). Shove the picks between the tiny mirror tiles.

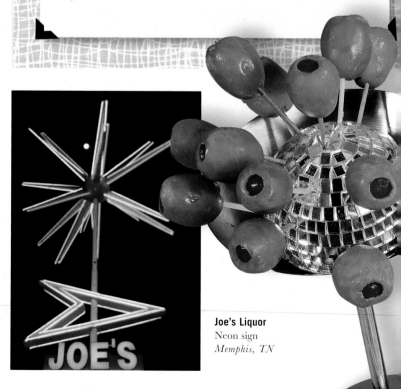

Joe's Liquor
Neon sign
Memphis, TN

Ooh La La
Lampshade

Materials

List of 4 to 6 French words

Paper doll accessories, or other paper cutouts

Scrap paper

White glue

Toothpicks

Lampshade

Glitter *(extra fine works best)*

Paper towels

2 pairs of pantyhose
(more for a large shade)

Thread

Tools

Medium-point felt marker

Tweezers

Brush for glue

Scissors

Needle

Less sheer hose with some support work well for this. The springiness gives the rosettes a little more snap, and the cut edges roll up for a nice finish.

Practice, then paint

1 Make a list of 4 to 6 words in French. If you're like me and you don't *parlez-vous Francais*, use a French/English dictionary or a translation program on the internet. I used boudoir-related words that described the paper doll accessories I chose to decorate the shade. *I didn't really know or care if they're technically accurate since I can't tell the difference, and they look cool to me. These were my words:*

Bijouterie Fantaisie (Junk Jewelry)
Eau de Toilette (Cologne)
Sac á Main (Handbag)
Houppe á Poudrer (Powder Puff)

2 Sketch curved lines on scrap paper, and practice writing the words along the curves using the felt marker. Words written on curves can wrap around the paper cutouts and overlap, if you run out of room. I looked at a vintage craft pamphlet with lots of hand-script type as a reference for my lettering style.

3 Squeeze out a small amount of white glue on scrap paper, dip a toothpick into it, and "write" a letter on the shade with the glue-tipped toothpick.

4 Immediately shake glitter onto your glue writing, and shake the excess off onto a piece of scrap paper.

Some pointers on glitter writing

- *In case you're thinking glitter glue would be a good shortcut for this project, no, no, Nanette! Glitter glue is too thick. The lettering may look gloppy and sag before it dries.*

- *Glue and glitter one letter at a time. It gives you the time to make each letter deliberately as you'd like without rushing, and without having to worry about the glue drying before you get the glitter on. Because you are applying tiny amounts of glue and possibly working on a porous surface (such as the fabric-covered shade pictured), it's easy to lose your place. If this happens, glitter whatever portion of the letter you have done and continue on.*

To slim down a letter that turns out thicker than you wanted, use the end of the tweezers to scrape off the excess glue. Wipe off the tweezers immediately with paper towels so they're ready for the next touch-up.

Glue cutouts

5 Decide where the cutouts are going on the shade. One at a time, brush white glue on the back of a cutout and put it in place. Dab over it gently with a wadded paper towel to help it stick. *Because I was working on a fragile fabric shade, I held a wad of paper towels behind each cutout as I dabbed to keep from damaging the shade's lining.*

Pantyhose "rosettes"

I got 16 rosettes from each pair of pantyhose. I used 36 pieces on this 7" shade

6 Cut the toes off of one of the pantyhose legs.

7 Tie a knot at the end of the leg, pulling down tight on the knot toward the cut end.

8 Cut the knot off of the pantyhose leg, leaving about an inch of unknotted hose on the end.

9 Pull on each end of the cut piece, away from the knot, to tighten it.

10 Pull the cut edges on the end of the knot down towards the knot, opening them up to form the rosette.

11 Continue knotting and cutting, first up the rest of that leg of the hose until you reach the panty, then up the other leg. Cut additional pairs of hose until you have enough rosettes to rim the shade.

12 Make tiny stitches in the knot of each rosette to tack it to the shade, trimming the top and the bottom.

Voilá! C'est magnifique!

Lizzy Faire, the Indifferent
Pantyhose Poodle

Materials

3 pink pipe cleaners:
  4 pieces, 1" each
  1 piece, 3"
  6 pieces, 4" each
  1 piece, 5"
4 skinny white pipe cleaners
  1 piece, 1"
  22 pieces, 2" each
1 skinny black pipe cleaner
  2 pieces, 1" each
Large artificial holly berry
Glossy black acrylic paint
Tacky craft glue
Glitter *(a couple flakes of red, gold, and copper)*
2 plastic foam balls, 2" dia.
3 plastic foam balls, 1" dia.
Doll eyelashes *(or cheap false eyelashes)*
Hot glue
1 pair pale pantyhose
Black felt
Metal bottle cap
2 bamboo skewers

Tools

Wire cutters
Paintbrush
Craft saw
Hot glue gun
Scissors

Poodle prep

1 Paint the holly berry gloss black. Set it aside to dry. *(If it's attached to a long wire, trim it down to 1".)*

2 Shake out a couple of flakes of the various colors of glitter. Put a dot of tacky craft glue on the end of a 1" piece of skinny white pipe cleaner, and dip it into the glitter. Set it aside.

3 Double up one of the 4" pieces of pink pipe cleaner for the neck. Push one end of it into the center of one of the 2" plastic foam balls. Push the other end of it into the center of the other 2" foam ball, leaving about 3/4" of it exposed to be the neck. It should look like a prissy barbell.

Get a leg up

4 To make her legs, push four 4" pieces of pink pipe cleaner into the underside of her body.

5 Saw the three teeny foam balls in half with the craft saw. Put two aside for now. To make her feet, push the curved side of a foam ball half onto the end of each leg.

Put a muzzle on it

6 Holding the barbell assembly vertical, push the end of a 2" skinny white pipe cleaner deep into the center of what will be her face *(either end of the prissy barbell)*. Push the flat side of one of the teeny foam ball halves onto the protruding bit of pipe cleaner till it's flush against the larger foam ball.

Eyes without a face

7 For each eye, put a dot of hot glue on the center of a 1" piece of skinny black pipe cleaner and press it on the top edge of the lashes, like velvety eyeliner. Bend back the very ends of the pipe cleaner and press the lashes in place on her face. Space her eyes at least 1/2" apart.

8 For puffy pink eyelids *(And what girl doesn't want those!)*, bend back the ends of four 1" pieces of pink pipe cleaner. For each eye, position one piece of pipe cleaner directly above the lashes, and press the ends into her face. Put another piece directly above that.

Ears, nose & smoke

9 To make an ear, bend a 5" piece of pink pipe cleaner in half, pinching together the loose ends, and pushing them into the head. Bend the ear down and then flip it up to shape it. Repeat with a 4" piece of pink pipe cleaner for the other ear.

10 Push the holly berry into the center of the muzzle to make her nose. *(If there's no wire attached, put a dot of hot glue on the end of it first.)*

11 Push the cigarette that you made in step 2 in place.

Groom your poodle

12 Cut across the panty hose legs to make strips:
    12 that are 1" tall (venti strips)
    16 that are 1/2" tall (grande)

13 Make pipe cleaner poofs as directed in the photo below. You will need:

6 pipe cleaner poofs made with venti pantyhose strips (1")

16 pipe cleaner poofs made with grande pantyhose strips (1/2")

Each is made on a 2" piece of skinny white pipe cleaner, so you will need 22 pieces to make these poofs.

14 Push the six large poofs in place:
    3 on top of her head
    3 on her chest

15 Trim the pipe cleaners on the 16 small poofs to be 1/4" long. Push four into each of her feet.

16 Tie two venti pantyhose strips to the loop on the end of each of her ears. Pull the knot tight. Clip with scissors to trim to about 1/2" long. Pull and fluff.

17 To make her tail, bunch up the two remaining venti pantyhose strips, and make a pipecleaner poof *(right)* using a 3" piece of pink pipe cleaner. Put it in place on her derriere.

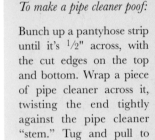

To make a pipe cleaner poof:

Bunch up a pantyhose strip until it's 1/2" across, with the cut edges on the top and bottom. Wrap a piece of pipe cleaner across it, twisting the end tightly against the pipe cleaner "stem." Tug and pull to make it poofy.

Make her French

18 Cut a 2 1/4" circle of felt for her beret. Use the scissor's blade to poke a small hole in the center of it.

19 Cut a thin strip of felt, about 2" long. Double it over and poke it through the hole in the felt to make a loop on top of her beret.

20 Put a ring of hot glue inside the bottle cap and wrap the felt around the cap. Use the bamboo skewers to push it into the glue. Hot glue it to her head, off to the side a little.

21 Clip any errant threads. Fluff her up. Bend her, shape her any way you want her, but I like her proud and jaunty.

Strike a Lucky Pose in a

Pillbox Party Hat

Materials

1 sheet of 11" x 17" cardstock

Decorative paper, 2½" x 17"

Glue stick

Paper or imagery to decorate the top

Hot glue

Thematic paper cutouts

Trim for the top edge of the hat (tinsel garland or roping are nice; a pipe cleaner will work too)

Sparkly pipe cleaner

Tinsel or other bling for the top of the antenna

Ornament for base of antenna

Elastic strap or hairpins

Tools

Pencil

Straightedge

Craft knife

Scissors

Hot glue gun

Wire cutters

A cutting mat is really handy for this project, if you have one.

Suzie Do

C**ostume** shops are a good source for elastic straps. You could also cannibalize a cheap mask. Or you can skip the strap altogether and use hairpins to hold the hat in place.✳

Prepare the base

1 Cut a strip from the cardstock, 2½" wide and 17" long. Set aside the rest of the sheet to use later.

2 Draw a line down the length of the strip you cut ½" in from the edge. Score it using the straightedge and the back of the craft knife. Fold it in towards the score. This will be the inside of the hat.

3 Turn the strip over so you're working on the outside. Beginning at the score, cover the entire front with decorative paper, wrapping it around the bottom edge and ½" deep on the inside. It should not cover the first ½" above the score. Use glue stick to cover the part of the front that will be covered with paper. Press and smooth the paper on the glue. Flip the strip over. Crease the overlap. Glue stick the inside edge, and press and smooth the overlap in place.

Make tabs to support the top

4 Flip the strip back to the front side. Holding the straightedge along the score with the un-papered ½" edge exposed, make tabs by cutting through the entire un-papered edge, from the score to the outside edge of the strip at 1" intervals down the entire length of the strip.

5 Bend the tabs down toward the inside of the hat.

Form the base

6 With the decorative paper on the outside, bring the two ends of the strip together, and hot glue them to each other with about an inch of overlap. You can adjust it gently if you think it needs to be rounded out some.

Make the top

7 Using the pencil, make two tracings of the circumference of the inside of the hat onto the reserved piece of cardstock.

8 Cut out the two almost-circles. One will be the outside top of the hat, and the other will be a reinforcement and finishing touch for the inside. The outer one will be edged with tinsel and the inner one is unseen, so don't worry if they're a little irregular.

9 Try putting one of the circles inside the hat. Trim the circle if it doesn't quite fit. Apply hot glue to the tabs inside the hat, and press the circle in place.

10 Decorate the top of the other circle. Hot glue it to the top of the hat.

Trim it till it's crazy cool

11 Use the glue stick to decorate the sides of the hat with the thematic paper cutouts.

12 Hot glue the trim to the top edge of the hat, covering the edge of the top circle.

Make & install the antenna

13 Cut the pipe cleaner to size, anywhere from 4 to 6" long. Stay on the short side if you plan to put anything besides tinsel on the top of the antenna. Double and twist the pipe cleaner if you add anything hefty.

14 Wrap the end of the pipe cleaner around a bit of tinsel to make a sparkly cluster for the top.

15 Prepare something from the scraps on your work desk—a small square of paper, a little ball of tinsel—to mount over the base of the antenna to reinforce it when it's hot glued to the hat.

16 Hot glue the base of the antenna to the center front of the hat, close to the bottom edge. Lay the prepared scrap over the glue. Add another bit of hot glue and press the ornament in place on top of the scrap.

Snap it on & look fabulous!

17 If you're using an elastic strap, with the seam in the back, poke a tiny cut on each side of the hat with the craft knife, just over ¼" up from the bottom edge. Push the ends of the elastic strap through the holes.

18 Snap that thing on your head. The party has started!

Quick as a wink

Glitter Critters

Start with a clean critter. It can be ceramic, plastic, plaster—anything that has a hard surface. Remove any trims—plastic eyes, chain collars, etc.—and put them aside. Choose some glitter. Micro glitter is easier to work with, but for old-school authenticity, chunky is funky. Pick an acrylic paint in a shade close to that of the glitter. Paint a thick coat on the critter. For anything other than a very small one, paint it in patches about the size of a sandwich cookie. Pour glitter over the wet paint. Continue until covered. If the critter has an opening on the bottom, insert a pencil or wooden dowel inside it to make a "handle" for holding while keeping your fingers out of the mess. Let the critter dry. Touch up any spots that need it. Cut some plastic flowers to make ridiculous eyelashes. Replace the original trims and eyes, or add some of your own. The deer pictured here were soft plastic, so I could push in some oversized animal eyes from the craft store, along with a large holly berry painted black for the nose. You can also accessorize with googly eyes, buttons, bells, ribbon, or whatever catches your fancy. This is a great way to resuscitate broken, cracked, and damaged animal pieces.

Bend! Fold! Spindle! Mutilate!

Paper is the handiest of all handicraft materials. You could be on a park bench in Bucharest, equipped only with a knowledge of paper chain making, and you could likely scrounge up enough paper to fashion yourself a small clutch purse, bracelet, box, or frame.

If you're gearing up to do some retro craft, start building a library of paper (see pages 43 and 44). If you have an aversion to clutter, set yourself a limit—a single drawer, storage tub, or shelf—and once that's full, collect only to restock what you've depleted.

Paper, Scissors, Craft Knife, Paper Cutter

Paper Cutting Essentials

Good paper scissors and a companion pair of plain scissors—For less than the cost of a sushi dinner, you can buy a pair of small, sharp scissors that will work like magic when cutting paper. If you haven't had a pair of precise, paper-designated scissors before, let me tell you, they will be life changing. Make a commitment to your paper scissors that you will never, ever use them to cut anything else. Wherever you keep them, keep a pair of plain, "dummy" scissors next to them, for cutting everything else. The dummy scissors will help you keep your commitment.

Folded paper project photos courtesy Amos Craft Publishing, Sidney, OH 45365 USA, From *Pack-o-Fun* magazine, January 1967 & April 1968

Paper chain objects were all the rage in the 1960s. Belts, purses, and frames were favorite projects. Cigarette packs and gum wrappers were the preferred materials—they could be folded so no cutting and trimming were required. (Maybe that's why so many prisoners made craft items from them, since scissors weren't necessary.)

Guillotine, or arm-trimmer paper cutter—These are pricey when you buy them new, but they do show up at yard sales or office supply resellers at rock-bottom prices. The most desirable ones have a hand clamp next to the blade to hold the paper in place, insuring better cuts.

Rotary trimmers and compact rotary trimmers—These little trimmers are an affordable alternative to guillotine cutters. They do a good job and the replacement blades are inexpensive, making upkeep practical. The compact versions are handy for packing in a kit and bringing along.

Craft knives, blades, straightedge, and a cutting mat—A craft knife is essential, but it's useless without a supply of new blades and a straightedge. For a straightedge, nothing beats the metal rules with nonslip cork backing.

I use #11 craft blades by the bucketful, so I buy them in boxes of 100 because it's way cheaper than buying them five at a time. I keep an upturned ceramic mug with a gritty, unglazed surface along the bottom to sharpen my blades (pull the blade across it on an angle, alternating from side to side like you would when sharpening a knife). Never hesitate to use a new blade when you're cutting vintage papers or anything requiring a lot of precision.

A large, self-healing cutting mat is very useful. Besides protecting surfaces, it prolongs the life of your blades. Mats can be pricey, and if you're not ready to make the plunge, a piece of corrugated cardboard will do. When cutting small things, I frequently use an old record album cover if the mat isn't handy.

Be Careful!

Use a craft knife with extreme care; they can do a lot of damage if used improperly. Two cardinal rules from Graphics 101:

1 Always keep your non-cutting hand out of harm's way—never, ever below the hand with the blade.

2 When using a metal straightedge and craft knife, always cut on the scrap side, using the rule to protect what you're planning to use. If the blade slips, and sometimes it does, it will damage the scrap.

Suzie Do

*H*ave a crazy thrift store painting you love, but maybe you, or someone else in your household covets the wallspace it's taking up? Take a digital photograph of it and print it out to fit a small frame. ✳

Caffeinated Paper Chain Frame

Materials

6 coffee bags
Heavy-duty thread
5" x 7" piece of cardstock or light board
5" x 7" image

Tools

Straightedge
Craft knife
Cutting surface
Needle
Scissors or nail clippers *(for trimming thread)*
Small-scale paper cutter is handy for cutting bags into pieces.

I used glossy plastic coffee bags because I liked the colors. But I realized quickly that folding made the strips too bulky, so instead I cut them to size. They're easier to work with, but the finished piece doesn't "poof" the way folded vintage pieces did. I like the svelte appearance.

Prep links

1 Pull coffee bags open along the seams. Clean and dry them. Flatten on cutting surface. Trim off any crimped, glued, or otherwise unusable portion of the bags *(including that weird little vent thing)*.

2 Cut the bags into 3½" pieces. Cut those pieces into ³⁄₈" wide strips. An average coffee bag yields 45 strips. The frame as pictured took 226 strips, including the 68 same-color strips that frame the back panel.

Make the strips

3 Make the strips following the directions in the How-to at right. You will need:

For the front:
2 strips, 9½ links long *(for the top and bottom)*
2 strips, 6½ links long *(for the sides)*

For the back:
2 strips, 10½ links long, all the same color *(for the top and bottom)*
2 strips, 7½ links long, all the same color *(for the sides)*
4 strips, 9½ links long *(to fill in)*

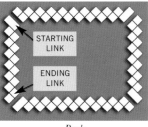

Back   *Front*

Frame-up

4 Assemble the back of the frame, connecting the strips for the top, bottom, and sides by making corners as described in the How-to.

5 Now that you've honed your corner skills, join the strips for the top, bottom, and sides of the frame front.

Get to stitchin'

6 Fill in the frame back by stitching in four strips, two directly below the top strip and two directly above the bottom strip, leaving a gap in the center to slip the image through.

7 Center the frame front on the frame back. Sew it in place along the outside edges, hiding the stitches so they aren't visible on the front. *(Keep stitches along the outside edges to avoid making any that will block the image from slipping inside the window space.)*

Put it together

8 Slip the cardstock backer and image into the frame through the gap in the back.

9 Make up a colorful story, attributing your handsome frame to an incarcerated family member.

The pieces used to make links can be any size as long as they're eight or nine times longer than they are wide.

To make links: Fold each piece in quarters—first fold in half end to end, then fold the ends in to the center, and crease folds tightly.

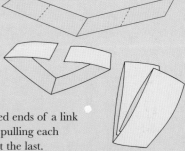

To make strips: Push the folded ends of a link through the loops of another link, pulling each consecutive new link tightly against the last.

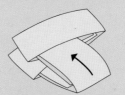

Keep in mind:
The starting link on every strip is never overlapped. When adding links to a strip, always add them to the other end.

To join strips: Use a needle and heavyweight thread. First, run the needle through one of the loops and tie a knot to secure the thread. "Stitch" two strips together by pulling the needle through loops, alternating between rows. *(See illustration right.)* The needle and thread snake through the loops, without actually piercing them. To add another strip, at the end of a row, pass the needle up through loops to the next row, and continue joining that strip to the next.

To make corners: *Each strip has a starting link on one end and an ending link on the other. (The starting link is the only link on the strip that is not overlapped.) Each corner should connect a starting link to an ending link (having two starting links on one corner will make that corner loose).*

Lay out the strips as shown in the illustrations for the front and back of the frame. *(Above left.)* Open up a link so it is doubled, and not quartered, and on each corner:

a. Slip the doubled link through the end link

b. Wrap it around the starting link

c. Tuck the ends into the center

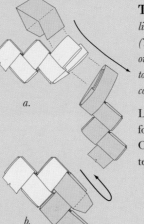

Wishing You Were Here
Postcard Frame

Materials

10" x 12" board
Scrap paper larger than board
Acrylic paint
6 to 10 postcards
2" x 3" picture frame
2 saw-tooth picture hangers
Image to frame
Tacky craft glue
Paper towels
4' of rickrack
4 buttons
Hot glue
1 small nail

Tools

Pencil
Paintbrush
Craft knife
Metal straightedge
Hammer
Scissors
Hot glue gun

Prep

1 Use the pencil to trace around the board onto the scrap paper. This will be your layout template.

2 Paint the board front, back, and sides. Set aside to dry.

Layout and trim

3 The postcards need to be set in from the edge of the board to leave room for trim. Draw a line ¹/₂" from the edge inside the template.

4 Lay out the postcards on this inner area of the template until you find an arrangement you like. Put the small frame on top of the design so you can see what it covers. The postcards don't need to completely cover the area underneath the frame, but they need to run at least ¹/₄" underneath it on all sides so there is no gap or uncovered wood showing.

5 Once you're absolutely crazy about the layout, use the craft knife and straightedge to trim any postcards that need to be cropped. (In the design pictured, only three cards were used without cropping.) Crop postcards one at a time, returning them to the template after they're trimmed so that you can see if everything is fitting together as expected (and so you don't forget your brilliant design).

Assemble

6 Attach one picture hanger to the center of the back of the small frame. Put the image in the frame.

7 When the board is dry, attach the other picture hanger to the back about 2" from the top and centered from the sides.

8 One at a time, take a postcard from the template, paint the back with tacky craft glue, and position it on the painted board. Cover the face of each postcard with a clean paper towel, and gently swirl your fingertips over to make sure all edges are pressed down well. Blot up any excess glue.

(I like to wing it, but if you prefer you can lightly draw your ¹/₂" inset on the board before you begin gluing cards.)

9 Cut four pieces of rickrack to cover the outside edges of the cards on each side of the frame. Glue it around the outside edges of the cards, wiping up any excess glue.

10 Hot glue the buttons in the corners, covering the ends of the rickrack.

11 Set the small frame in place. Press down and wiggle it a little to make the hanger dig into the board and leave a mark; this is where the small nail will go. Hammer in the nail and set the frame in place. If you don't foresee ever wanting to change the image in the frame, you could hot glue the frame in place. That requires careful measuring and leveling, so I stick with the sawtooth hanger.

variations

Try other trims! This vacation photo inspired glossy road-trip-themed postcards and shiny red and yellow thumbtacks. The small inner frame is trimmed with covers from souvenir matchbooks, scraps of postcards, and glossy red strips cut from a coffee bag using scalloped scissors.

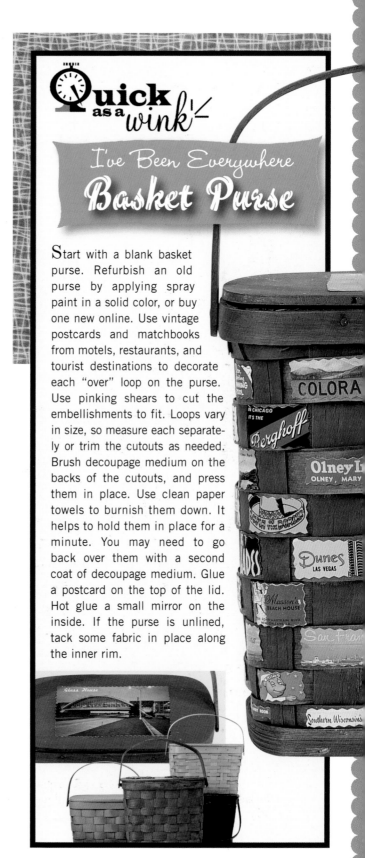

Quick as a wink!

I've Been Everywhere Basket Purse

Start with a blank basket purse. Refurbish an old purse by applying spray paint in a solid color, or buy one new online. Use vintage postcards and matchbooks from motels, restaurants, and tourist destinations to decorate each "over" loop on the purse. Use pinking shears to cut the embellishments to fit. Loops vary in size, so measure each separately or trim the cutouts as needed. Brush decoupage medium on the backs of the cutouts, and press them in place. Use clean paper towels to burnish them down. It helps to hold them in place for a minute. You may need to go back over them with a second coat of decoupage medium. Glue a postcard on the top of the lid. Hot glue a small mirror on the inside. If the purse is unlined, tack some fabric in place along the inner rim.

Twilight Time
Starburst
Clock

Materials

Black cardstock
Scrap paper
Metallic paint
12 bamboo skewers
Black acrylic paint
2 round papier-mâché box lids
(5" and 6" pictured)
Hot glue
Quartz clock movement and hands
Battery

Tools

Pencil
Straightedge
Craft knife
Paintbrush
Old toothbrush
Rag
Hot glue gun
Drill

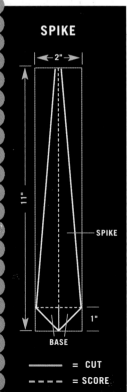

SPIKE

← 2" →

11"

SPIKE

1"

BASE

——— = CUT
- - - - = SCORE

Clock mechanisms come in different hand-shaft lengths. This one is ⅞", but yours may need to be larger or smaller depending on the lids you use.

Make the spikes

1 Cut 12 pieces of black cardstock, 2" x 11". The 11" edge should run with the grain *(see next page)*.

2 Cut and score each piece according to the illustration at left.

Paint

The scored side of the spike is the front. Work on scrap paper, starting with a fresh sheet for each spike so the other side stays clean.

3 For each spike, fold the two base tabs up against the back, then fold the spike back along the center score so that only one half of the front is exposed.

4 Brush metallic paint on the left side of each spike.

5 Open the spikes and spatter paint on the right side of each. (*Old toothbrushes are perfect for spattering. The bristles should be dry and dipped in a very small amount of paint; pull them back with one finger and let them go. Set the spikes upright beforehand for even coverage.*)

6 Fold the rag a couple of times to make a thick pad, and pour a little of the metallic paint onto it. Rub it onto the bamboo skewers. (*It's easy to get splinters so be sure the rag is thick.*)

7 Paint the interior of both lids black. Paint the sides of both lids, the top rim of the small lid, and the back of the large lid with metallic paint.

Form the spikes

8 For each spike, apply hot glue to the front of the left base panel. Gently bend the spike back along the scores, overlapping the right base panel over the left until it is aligned directly over it. Press and hold for a second.

Assemble the base

9 Hot glue the papier-mâché lids back to back, with the small lid centered against the large. Avoid gluing the very center. (*That would make the next step harder.*)

10 Drill a hole in the exact center of the small lid. It needs to be large enough to put the clock mechanism through.

11 Install the clock movement and hands following the package directions. (*This set had a washer that made a nice finishing touch over the hole on the clock face.*)

12 Install the battery to be sure the clock is assembled correctly, then take it out.

Spike it

13 Apply hot glue evenly to the base of one of the spikes and press it on the outside of the small lid, in the 12 o'clock position. Add spikes at 3, 6, and 9 o'clock.

14 Place the rest of the spikes, two between each of the initial spikes.

15 Put a little hot glue on the large lid, behind and between two spikes. Stick the blunt end of a bamboo skewer in the glue, and hold till firm. Continue with the rest of the skewers.

16 Pop the battery in and get your terrific timepiece up on the wall.

Using light materials and hot glue make this clock go together in no time. It also makes it fragile, so handle with care.

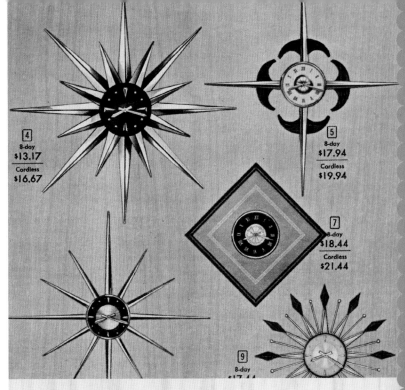

Grain

Paper is made of fiber. The direction that most of those fibers run in determines the paper's grain. The heavier the paper, the more obvious the grain.

Determining the grain

The fold test—If you have an extra piece of the paper you plan to use, or can afford to clip an inch square corner off the sheet of paper, this is the easiest way to figure out the direction of the grain. (If you clip a little square, clip a tiny notch in the upper right-hand corner so you'll know the orientation. Fold the sample paper once in each direction. The cleaner fold indicates the direction of the grain.

The bend test—Hold the paper with a hand on each side. Without creasing, bend the two sides toward each other. Now do the same with the top and bottom of the paper. The direction that offers the least resistance indicates the direction of the grain.

The droop test (especially effective with medium-weight papers)— Put the sheet of paper on the edge of a table. Note how much it droops. Turn it a quarter turn so that what was the top is now hanging off the edge, and note the droop. The paper will droop more when the grain is parallel to the table edge.

If, after testing, it's not apparent which direction the grain is going, it probably isn't strong enough to affect how the paper works in your project.

45 rpm
Record Tote

Once the panels are cut, the underlying box goes together fast and easy using gummed kraft paper tape. I don't worry about the tape being non-archival, or that the panels aren't glued; the decorative paper and decoupage medium add an additional strength, an exoskeleton, that make the box sturdy.

Materials

Heavy cardboard
(see Cut List on page 71 for details)
Gummed kraft paper tape
Tacky craft glue
Vintage magazines *(or other source of fun imagery)*
Waxed paper
Scrap paper
Paper towels
Decoupage medium
1 sheet of tissue paper
4 index cards
4 purse feet or rubber feet *(optional)*
Handle
2 small hinges
Snap catch or other closure for the front
36" long 1" wide strip of fabric trim
(feathery marabou is my favorite; felt, foam, or other trims will work too)

*C*heck home centers, art, hobby, and fabric stores for small hardware made especially for using on small boxes or purses. There's a lot more available on the web. Search for "purse handles," "purse supplies," "cigar box purse supplies," "craft hardware," and "small hinges."

Tools

Pencil
Craft knife
Straightedge
Scissors
Sponge
Rag
2 to 3 medium foam brushes
6 small clamps *(large binder clips will work)*
Drill *(hand or electric)*
Screwdriver

Cardboard Cut List

2 pieces 8" x 7" *(front and back panels)*

2 pieces 5" x 7" *(side panels)*

1 piece 5" x 8" *(bottom panel)*

1 piece 10½" x 7½" *(lid)*

1 piece 26" x 1¼" *(lid guide)*

1 piece 5" x 2" *(handle reinforcement strip)*

side	front	side	back

| | bottom | | |

Day 1

Make the box

1 Cut out the panels detailed in the Cut List.

2 Arrange the panels as shown above. Leave a little, tiny gap between the panels so they'll flex when taped. Tape the seams on one side, then flip everything over and tape the other side.

3 Stand the taped panels up, with the bottom panel in place underneath. Bring together the back and side panel that have not been taped. Tape that seam, inside and out. Tape the three untaped seams on the bottom panel, first inside and then out.

Make the lid

Look at the sketch on the Cut List to visualize what you're going to do next.

4 To make the sides of the lid, cut a 1¼" square out of each corner of the lid panel.

5 Score the cardboard as indicated by the dotted lines in the sketch.

6 Bend the sides of the lid down along the scores and tape the seams, inside and out.

7 Glue the handle reinforcement strip to the inside center of the lid.

Plan imagery

8 Choose a theme, and find imagery. Clip more than you need, then pick and choose what works best together. Consider the visual flow from the lid to the box, and from each panel to the next. Clip imagery for the underside of the box and for the inside of the box and lid.

Decoupage till delirium

9 Lay a long strip of waxed paper on your work surface to keep your work from sticking to it. Ready a stack of scrap paper, a damp sponge, a roll of paper towels, and a damp rag to wipe your hands on.

10 Choose an image from the underlayer of the design. Lay it facedown on a sheet of scrap paper, and brush decoupage medium on the back. Press it in place on the box, using the damp sponge to press out any air bubbles or wrinkles. The clippings are fragile when they're soggy, so be gentle. Start with the interior, and work your way to the outside, and then the lid. Repeat with the remaining clippings. Allow to dry overnight.

Day 2

Seal the deal

11 Paint the outside of the lid and box with decoupage medium. Allow to dry according to the directions for the medium you're using.

Lid guide

12 Measure the inside dimensions of your box. Score the lid guide strip to wrap around the inside edge of the box. Trim tissue paper to cover it. Brush decoupage medium on the guide strip, cover it with tissue, then bend the strip to fit inside the box while the medium is still damp (so that the tissue will stretch and not break).

13 Brush glue on the inside edge of the box, and put the lid guide in place, with the top edge about ⅜" above the rim and the ends toward the back. Clamp in place. (Put folded index cards over the rim of the box and under the clamp to protect the imagery.)

Install hardware

Hardware installation will vary according to what you use. For anything that will be screwed on, hold the hardware in place and mark the screw holes with a pencil. Drill holes smaller than the screws with a hand or electric drill.

14 Make slits for the purse feet, about ¾" in from the edges on all four corners of the bottom of the box. Push them in place.

15 Put the handle on the lid, the hinges on the back of the lid and box (about 1" in from the outside edges), and the front clasp on the center of the lid and box.

16 Add a trim to the lid guide to cover any hinge hardware exposed on the inside of the box.

17 Fill your box with your very favorite 45s, or give it to someone you really, really like.

Crazy for Christmas

The holidays have been crazy sparkly since the first lantern-swinging pinecone elf set sail from Japan to land on the shelf at a five-and-dime. Maybe that's why the holidays are the one time when the non-craft enthused cut the rest of us some slack. We can glitter and spangle to our hearts' content without anyone worrying that we went off our meds.

I have been crazy for Christmas and all the holly-jolly craft it brings for my entire life. I live in the frosty-loggy-piney-elfy-snowy wonderland in my head. This section features some of my favorites.

Christmas All Over Again

One of the best sources for supplies is old holiday decor. Pieces that are too tattered for display are perfect to put in the supply box to await reincarnation. Vintage holiday decorations can be found in antique malls, flea markets, and even some thrift stores year-round. (It takes a little training to notice holiday decor when you're not in the mistletoe mindset.) On the internet, it's there 24-7, 365.

When junking, look for holiday decor with an eye toward disassembling it. Plastic holly wreaths are packed with holiday bang for your buck. In addition to the foliage, they're often spiked with small ornaments and other reusable decorations. Look for tiny deer and pine trees in ornaments and centerpieces you'd otherwise have no interest in. And strings of holiday lights you wouldn't dare plug into an outlet can have fabulous reflectors, tin and plastic, that are an absolute must for your retro holiday craft supply cabinet. Keep the bulbs, too.

Hoppy Holiday
Reinbeer!

One hot summer day, I used a craft knife to slice open a 12-pack. I was hoping to make a handy fridge dispenser, but instead I cut open three cans, making a not-so-handy beer fountain. Cans are much flimsier than they used to be. Tin snips are only needed to cut the rim while the rest of the can is easily cut with household scissors.

Materials

Beer can or other aluminum can, rinsed and dry
Template from page 170 copied on paper
Glue stick
Hot glue
White glue
Glitter
2 pipe cleaners
Floral berry for nose
Googly eyes *(7mm oval pictured)*

Tools

Tin snips
Scissors
Hot glue gun
Brush for glue
Small bowl or can for glitter
Awl or craft knife

Prep the can

1 Use tin snips to cut a slit in the reinforced rim on the top of the can about $^1/_2$" deep. Repeat on the opposite side.

2 Insert a scissor blade through the slit. Cut around the top of the can to remove it.

3 Cut down one side of the can until just before it tapers off on the bottom. Then cut off the bottom of the can as you did the top.

4 You should have a wobbly rectangle now. Trim any rough spots off the edges. You don't have a lot of can to work with, so just trim the ragged bits, don't worry about the rectangle being a little out of whack.

Paste, fold, and decorate

5 Loosely trim the template from the copy page. Use the glue stick to attach it to the unprinted side of the can.

6 Cut along the solid lines of the template using scissors. Don't miss the cut directly above the chest flap.

7 Fold the flaps, and then make the crease in the head.

8 Hot glue the back, bottom, and chest flaps closed.

9 Brush white glue on the ears and tail, and dip them in a small container of glitter.

10 To make the antlers, fold one pipe cleaner in half. Cut the other pipe cleaner into six pieces, each 2" long. Wrap three pieces around each half of the bent pipe cleaner, turning the ends up slightly (refer to the photo).

11 Glue the antlers in place. Hold the Reinbeer upside down, put the glue gun through the opening on the back of the neck, and put a puddle of hot glue into the area behind the face. Put the folded end of the antlers into the glue puddle, and hold a minute until set.

12 Hot glue the flap on the back of the neck closed.

13 Splay out the legs slightly, and arrange the antlers till the Reinbeer stands comfortably. Spread the ears out a little.

14 Glue on the nose. Make a small hole in the floral berry using the awl or craft knife. Put a dot of hot glue in the hole, and push the berry onto the end of the pointy snout.

15 This is where the Reinbeer comes alive. Put a dot of white glue on the back of each of the googly eyes, and press them in place. *Hoppy holidays!*

Quick as a **wink**

Tin Can Tree

A wispy tin-can tree can decorate the top of a package or join a forest of friends on the mantle. I like to have trimmed can panels handy around the studio. If you don't have any panels prepared, cut two cans open according to the directions above. Hot glue half of a plastic foam ball to an unfinished round wood base. Brush the top of it with white glue, and sprinkle on chunky white glitter. Fringe can panels and wrap them around dowels, attaching with glue dots. Top with a bit of tinsel, a tiny star, or a small glass ornament.

It takes a
Christmas
Village

Copying these templates onto cardstock takes all the measuring out of building a village. Just cut, score, and decorate!

The templates are laid out on a grid to make design changes easy. You could choose to make the windows one square long instead of two, make a building taller or shorter, thinner or wider, change the roof line, all without picking up a ruler.

The grid used is ¼", but you can copy these buildings to be as big or little as you'd like them to be.

Materials

Templates from page 170 copied on yellow cardstock
Vintage wrapping or other decorative papers
Glue stick
Scraps of colored transparent film *(sold new in rolls with gift-basket supplies in craft stores)*
Scraps of foil wrapping paper or other colorful foil
White glue
Hot glue
Toothpicks

Tools

Scissors
Craft knife
Straightedge
Small bowl
Hot glue gun
Small brush for glue
Paintbrush

Useful but optional: Paper edgers (shaped scissors) and a cutting mat

Additional materials when the mini house on the template is paired with the cottage as pictured (far left in photo):

2¼" length of a ³⁄₁₆" x 1" balsa plank
White acrylic paint
Iridescent glitter
Bit of white tinsel garland
1½" piece of white pipe cleaner
Bead or other ornament

It actually did take a village to build this village— my craft group worked on it collectively. By working as a group, we pooled our resources: wraps, films, and foils. We mixed and matched to make little buildings that each had its own character, but also fit well together. It's a great way to use scraps of vintage papers that seem too tiny to be useful, yet too beautiful to throw out. If you have a hard time finding an unblemished piece to cover an entire pattern, use smaller pieces trimmed to meet at the seams, or use chimneys and trims to cover flaws.

First things

1 Rough cut the template pieces from the cardstock (about $1/4$" from the solid cut line). By rough cutting now, you waste less decorative paper and save yourself the time and trouble of having to cut carefully twice.

2 Glue stick the blank side of the pattern pieces for the buildings and roofs to the backside of the decorative papers. Put the pattern pieces for chimneys, shutters, and awnings aside in a little bowl so they don't get lost with the scraps. You can decide how you want to decorate them after the buildings start to take shape.

Let the sunshine in

3 Cut out the openings for the windows and doors. Cut out the buildings. Cut out the roofs. *The round windows pictured were made with a handheld punch after the buildings were cut out.*

4 Cut out little scraps of colored film and foil slightly larger than the windows and doors. Put a small amount of white glue on a scrap of cardstock. Brush a little around the openings on the inside of the buildings, then press the film and foil in place. *None of the film or foil should overlap the dotted lines where the folds will be.*

Make like a tiny carpenter

5 Score all the dotted lines on the patterns with the backside of the craft knife.

6 Fold along all the dotted lines.

7 Assemble the buildings, and hot glue the seam tabs to hold them together.

8 Hot glue the tabs for the roofs and put the roofs in place.

Make like a tiny decorator

9 Pull out your bowl of bits. Decorate the chimney and awning pieces with colorful scraps. Brush white glue on the cardstock, and smooth the decorative papers in place. Wait until the glue is dry before trimming. *(We trimmed our awnings with scalloped-edge scissors.)* Score and fold. Hot glue in place.

10 Add shutters. You can probably just snip them without measuring; use the pattern if you like. Attach with white glue.

If adding the mini house to the cottage:

Base: Paint the balsa plank white. Sprinkle some glitter on it.

Tree: Hot glue a piece of white garland to the $1^{1}/2$" piece of pipe cleaner, leaving a little pipe cleaner sticking out of the bottom to push into the base. Remove the tree from the base, add a drop of hot glue to the hole, and replace the tree. Add a drop of white glue to the top of the tree, and add a bead or ornament.

There are endless ways to put a new spin on this project. Use pages from a children's picture book to make an adorable gift box that's sure to be treasured. Instead of gluing the roof, add a small piece of tape to attach it to the inside. Glue a checker or nickel (as pictured) to work as a small weight to keep the lid closed.

Turn to the next page for a variation that uses Christmas record album covers.

Look no further than the record bin at your local thrift store for retro-craft inspiration, and crafting material!

variation

Oh, Come, All Ye Percy Faithful
Christmas Record Album Village

Copy the templates from page 170 on clear acetate. Cut out all the pieces along the cut lines, including the windows and doors. For the buildings and roofs, put the clear patterns on the album covers and choose how you'd like to crop them. Trace all the outlines with a marker, including windows and doors. Cut out the openings for the windows and doors. Decorate them as described in step 4 on the previous page. Because the album covers are on heavy stock, you'll need to score the front side. Refer to the pattern for placement, and use the straightedge to make the scores. Assemble the buildings. Hot glue them together. Add details. These look great hung on the tree.

I added crisp white gingerbread trim, made by clipping white paper with scalloped scissors.

Perky
Pinecone Elf

Materials

White cardstock
Pinecone
Hot glue
Bumpy pipe cleaner
1" plastic foam ball
Pipe cleaners
Artificial holly berries
Decorative paper
Pom-pom
Tacky craft glue
Bead eyes *(found in the doll aisle at craft stores)*
3/8" piece of red yarn
Trims

This is a simple cousin in the vast, varied family of pinecone folk. He was made from a pre-frosted cone glued to corrugated white cardstock, branch side down. His hat is made from origami paper and a tinsel pipe cleaner.

Tools

Pencil
Scissors
Hot glue gun
Wire cutters
CD to trace around

The base-ics

1 Make a base for the pinecone elf by drawing a 1 1/2" circle on the cardstock and cutting it out.

2 Hot glue the pinecone to the cardstock base. It can go branch side up or down.

3 Cut a piece of bumpy pipe cleaner in half with wire cutters. Attach it to the top of the pinecone by pinching together the narrow portion in the middle and either twisting or gluing that to the back of the cone. Pull the bumpy ends from the back to the front of the pinecone, and shape them to be arms.

4 Put a puddle of hot glue on top of the cone, pause a second or two to let it cool just a little, and press the plastic foam ball into it firmly.

5 Bend a couple of small bits of pipe cleaner into U-shapes for shoes. Hot glue the open ends up against the pinecone on the base. Trim with holly berries, if you like.

Make a hat and face

6 Trace around the CD onto the back of the decorative paper. Cut out the circle, and cut that circle in half. Imagine that half is three slices of pizza. Cut off one slice. Wrap the remaining two pieces around to form a cone-shaped hat. (The point will be on the straight edge, the opening will be on the curved edge.) Put a spot of hot glue on the back to hold it together.

7 Run a bead of hot glue around the inside rim of the hat, and glue it to the foam head.

8 Trim a piece of pipe cleaner to fit around the base of the hat. Put a bead of hot glue around the outside bottom edge, and wrap the pipe cleaner around it.

9 Hot glue a pom-pom to the top of the hat.

10 Use a holly berry for the nose. Put a tiny bit of tacky craft glue on the back of the nose and the eyes, and press them into place. *(Hot glue melts plastic foam, so unless you're really confident in your hot glue technique, stick with the tacky craft glue for critical detail work.)*

11 Pull a single thread from the piece of red yarn. Trim it to size. Put a little tacky craft glue on the back, and put it in place as a smile.

Personalize your piney person

12 Add some special trim. Classic Christmas elf accessories include lanterns, musical instruments, and little cardboard skis and wire poles. *My elf is hoisting a miniature reproduction of my favorite Christmas single.*

Fabulous
Ribbon Tree

Materials

Templates from pages 171 copied onto cardstock
3/4" satiny gift ribbon in 3 colors, at least 8' of each
Roll of wrapping paper *(coordinate with the ribbon)*
Transparent tape
Glue stick
1/2" double-sided tape
Decoration for the top
Hot glue *(optional)*

Tools

Pencil
Craft knife
Straightedge
Scissors
Hot glue gun *(optional)*

This project requires a little time, but very little concentration. The tree is three sided, with a fourth panel that slips behind another to make it sturdier and easier to work on. You'll be putting together a cardstock form, covering it in wrapping paper, making it fabulous with shimmering pieces of ribbon, and topping it with something flashy. Use a storebought topper, or make one yourself: fast and easy, a little ball of tinsel garland or a glass ornament. A mini sputnik is not as fast, but lots of fun.

Cut out the templates

1 Cut out both pieces of the tree from the copy sheet.

2 Cut out the handy *Ribbon Spacer* from the template, and set it aside with the ribbon.

Cut out decorative paper

3 Trace around one of the tree pieces onto the back of the wrapping paper. Fold the wrapping paper to yield two panels when you cut. Cut them out, and put the cut pieces aside for a minute. Get that clumsy roll of wrap out of your way.

Assemble the tree

4 Score the dotted lines on the tree pieces using the straightedge and the backside of the craft knife blade.

5 Crease folds, folding in toward the scored side.

6 Crease the wrap pieces by lining up the tree pieces on top of them and re-creasing the folds. Set the wrap aside.

7 Stand up the two creased tree pieces. Bring them together, overlapping the panel of one tree piece under the panel of the other tree piece (it doesn't matter which) to make a three-paneled tree.

8 Wrap your hand around them both, about 3" from the top, and tape them together securely with transparent tape.

9 Apply glue stick to one piece of wrap. The finished tree will be stronger and look tidier if you position the wrap so that it straddles the seam where the two pieces of the tree join without the overlap. Attach the wrap to the tree, pressing down to make contact. It might help to put your hand up the tree for support. Apply glue stick to the other piece of wrap, and attach it.

Make it fabulous

10 This is where the handy *Ribbon Spacer* becomes handy. Use it to mark the tree, drawing lines from side to side, 1" apart. On each side, line up the spacer on the bottom edge and draw 12 lines, stopping about 4" shy of the top.

11 Cut a pile of 2" lengths from one color of ribbon. It takes about 45 pieces of 3/4" ribbon to cover each side of the tree.

12 Fringe each piece of ribbon. Make four cuts from one end of the short edge towards the other, stopping short of the last 1/2". I like to curl the ribbon after fringing it by dragging the face of it between my thumb and a scissor blade. It distresses the finish on some ribbons, but I still like it. The fringe is fine flat, too.

13 On one side of the tree, put a strip of double-sided tape just under each of the lines. When you reach the unlined top of the tree, run two long strips of double-sided tape vertically, from the tip to about 1/4" shy of the topmost line.

14 Starting at the bottom of the tree, cover each strip of tape with fringed ribbon pieces. On some rows, the last ribbon will hang off the edge a little; pull a single fringe or two off to make them fit. When you reach the vertical tape at the top of the tree, make the ribbon in each row slightly shorter than in the last, ending up with a 1" piece at the very top.

15 Continue with the other sides, one at a time. (*Taping all sides at once makes the tree hard to work on, and the tape gets icky.*)

16 Crown that jewel! Top your tree with something spectacular. (*I leave the topper unglued so it's easier to store. If you use a glass ornament that you're afraid might break if it fell off, or if you just prefer, hot glue the topper in place. Geeze, I love these things.*)

Mini Sputnik
Holiday Style

Use a 1" plastic foam ball, toothpicks (round or flat), and one bamboo skewer. Follow the Sputnik directions on page 54, or just jam a jillion toothpicks into the foam ball (not too deep; it'll break apart). Put the bamboo skewer in first to make it easier to handle, and to help keep it anchored on the finished tree. Spray paint the assembled Sputnik, and shake on a healthy amount of glitter. For a frosty Sputnik, spray paint it white, give it an ample coat of spray snow, and while it is still wet, dip the tips in a bowl of iridescent glitter. Oooh, so sparkly!

Encrustations

Retro crafters love encrusting. Beads, shells, buttons, bottlecaps, wooden spools, matchsticks, artificial flowers, aquarium gravel, eggshells, macaroni, and all forms of pasta show up on just about anything a retro crafter can get his Elmer's on.

Encrustation works with a little or a lot. Let the degree to which you are obsessive be your guide. If you are able to make pieces accented with partial areas of encrustation, explore that, relishing your capacity for restraint. If you can't stop until there's not a single solitary speck of the original object showing, kudos to you for your thoroughness.

What to Encrust?

Boxes, jars, plates, figurines, foam balls, shoes—just about anything can be encrusted. Blemished things with cracks, scratches, or tears are good candidates. The encrustation process transforms them from damaged goods to fabulosity.

"Do you want to use natural coloring or something thrillingly unnatural?"

Recommended Adhesives

LIGHTWEIGHT ENCRUSTATIONS:
Tacky craft glue

MEDIUM-WEIGHT ENCRUSTATIONS:
Jewelry glue or silicone

HEAVY ENCRUSTATIONS:
Silicone or epoxy

Think twice before grabbing your glue gun for encrustation. Hot glue has a tendency to pop off of non-porous surfaces, and the stringy threads can be a nightmare.

I used brown-tinted silicone to encrust this whiskey bottle with aquarium gravel and paper cutouts.

Color Choices

Think about color before you begin gluing. Do you want to use natural coloring or something thrillingly unnatural?

Buttons, rocks, beads, and shells are great used "as is" without painting. They can be applied as a devil-may-care hodgepodge, or more deliberately in a limited palette of colors, or in a pattern.

If you opt for "unnatural" (and many retro crafters did—metallic gold being a favorite), encrust like crazy, and then spray paint the creation in one color. If you want to use more than one color, paint the encrustations before you glue them on.

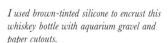

A Few General Rules of Encrustation

Work on waxed paper

Whenever you're encrusting, put waxed paper between the object and whatever surface you're working on. The paper protects the work surface, while the wax keeps the encrustation from sticking to the paper.

One side at a time

Light encrustations hold immediately when placed in the adhesive. You can keep the object upright while gluing, moving immediately from one side/area to the next. Heavy stuff slides off, so you have to tip the object on its side, glue the encrustations on, and wait for that side/area to dry before moving on to the next. (With delicate encrustations like seashells and pasta, pad the surface you lay the object on. An old towel or fabric remnant will do, and don't neglect to put a sheet of waxed paper between your fabulous encrusted thing and the padding.)

A Few Notes on Shells

Finding the quantity, color, and type of shells I like to have handy for projects requires more than a walk on the beach. Accumulating shells over time from thrift stores

and yard sales is a good way to start a collection. Notice them when they're not being offered as shells. Look for cheap jewelry and plant hangers made from shells, and ugly glass lamps or decorative jars full of them. If you find yourself needing shells in a hurry, the internet has the best selection and prices.

I sort shells into general categories and store them in plastic tubs. When I work on a shell project, I load up a tray with bowls and run down the line of tubs cafeteria style, picking out what I might need. Keeping them sorted in bowls makes it easy to put back what I don't use.

Macaroni Memories

(The Power of Pasta)

As frivolous as a towering, gold, macaroni Christmas tree may seem, like all retro craft, it can possess a gravity that its simple construction belies. As a grade schooler, I labored over a cardstock cone till every inch of it was covered with pasta. The gold spray paint transformed it, and I'm pretty sure I skipped all the way home to show it to my Mom. After a couple of days in a place of honor on the piano, my parents took it with them to leave in my Grandfather's room. He was in a long-term care facility—a facility I wasn't allowed to visit. I was disappointed that I would never see my macaroni masterpiece again, but remember a sense of pride that it would be with him when I couldn't. It was my connection to my grandfather during the long time he was away, and to this day, I can't see a macaroni tree without thinking of him.

Partially Encrusted

Trinket
Box

Materials

Interesting box
Shells
Plastic flowers
Mirror
Jewelry glue
Scraps of cardstock
Bamboo skewers
Glitter

Tools

Pencil
Scissors

Plan & lay out

1 Give a little thought to what kind of a look you want the finished piece to have, and what era you want it to convey. *(This delicate little powder box said "elegant, feminine, 1950s." To make it look older, the plastic flowers could be replaced with cloth flowers from a vintage hat. To make it look newer, it could be made with bolder colors and less delicate, more fanciful flowers.)*

2 Create a design for the shells and flowers. You can lay them directly on the lid or a flat surface, moving them around to come up with something you like. Or you can sketch a design on scrap paper. *(The intricate design on the lid of this box was laid out directly on the lid, then lifted and glued into place one piece at a time. Don't forget to create a design for the sides, also.)*

3 Be sure to plan some "breathing room." Part of the beauty of the partially encrusted object is choosing something interesting to work with and letting some of that original object show through.

Get to gluing

4 If you plan a mirror for your design, glue it on first. *(There's a 1" round mirror on the top center of the box pictured.)*

5 Squeeze a little glue onto scrap cardstock. Dip a bamboo skewer in the glue, and dab it onto the box. Push an encrustation into the glue. Continue dabbing glue and adding encrustations. If you want to reposition something, use a dry skewer to scoot things around without getting glue on your fingers.

6 For a large area that's less intricate, like the sides of the box pictured, you can use a scrap of cardstock to squeegee glue onto a wide patch of the box. Only cover as much area as you can encrust before the glue starts to dry.

The finishing touch

7 Wherever you want glitter, shake it into the wet glue or add more glue to specific areas. *(Chunky flakes of aqua glitter were sprinkled onto the lid, and little puddles of glue were added to the edges of the mini clamshells in the center to catch even more.)*

The rosettes on the bottom rim of this box are made with pearly mini umbonium shells, framed by amber pearled triangle trocus mini shells, and golden leaves made from the petals of the same kind of plastic flowers used to decorate the top.

Materials

  Wooden box *(cigar box shown)*
  Split spools
  Spray paint in two colors
  Waxed paper
  Epoxy or wood glue

The antique piece that inspired this was made with split spools, wooden spools that look like they've been cut in half vertically. I'm not sure if they were manufactured that way, but I was surprised to see that you can buy them. Search online, under "wood craft supplies split spools." This project has a pre-atomic age rural feel to it, so I chose an odd color combination I felt worked with that.

Old School

Split Spool Planter

Plan

1 Arrange the spools on the wooden box to figure out how many you will need to cover it. Alternate them vertically and horizontally. On the corners, I chose to have the horizontal spools meet horizontal spools, and vertical spools meet vertical spools. *(There are 54 spools used on the 9" x 5" box pictured.)*

2 Count how many vertical and how many horizontal spools are used in your design.

3 Makes notes or sketch your layout if you think you need to. Remove the spools from the box.

Paint

4 Put down waxed paper for painting the spools. Spray paint the horizontal spools one color and the vertical spools the other color. *(I like to paint a few extras in case I counted wrong.)* Let them dry.

Glue

5 Put the spools back on the box and arrange your design, distributing the space between spools and the space between rows of spools evenly so there are no large gaps. Glue them down.

Bless Your Pea-Pickin'
Candy Dish

Materials

Clear dish, with a lid
Picture
Self-adhesive felt
Split peas, lots and lots of split peas
Small glue dots
Spray paint for interior color
Antique white spray paint
Rag

Tools

Pencil
Scissors
Rag

I chose the glass dish used in this project because no matter where I travel, there's one of these things on the shelf at the local thrift store. Seriously. The junk world is lousy with them.

Prep

1 Use the bottom of the dish as a template. Trace around it on an image, and cut the image out. The image will be backed by felt, so you can use one from almost any source *(book, magazine, photograph, greeting card, wrapping paper, etc.)*. It's a secret little extra that can only be seen when the dish is empty.

2 Cut out a piece of felt about a 1/4" larger than the picture on all edges. *(This extra edge that extends beyond the image is what will hold the image to the dish.)*

3 Glue peas all over the dish and the lid by pressing each pea on a glue dot, then pressing it onto the dish. Space the peas evenly, about 1/2" apart. It's fun. Really.

4 Pull the paper backing off the felt. Set the felt aside. Dampen the backing and stick it over the bottom of the dish to work as a mask when you paint.

Paint

This project requires a very light touch with the spray paint. Be sure to hold the can at least 10" away from the dish, and spray a light coat each time.

5 Put the dish upside down and the lid right side up. Spray the outside of both with the interior color. *(This coat will show through the glass inside the dish.)*

6 When the interior coat is completely dry, spray the lid and dish with antique white paint.

Decorate the dish bottom

7 When the dish is thoroughly dry, remove the paper mask. Use the rag to clean up any paint that may have seeped through.

8 Center the picture over the felt, and stick the back-side of the picture onto the adhesive side of the felt.

9 Press the felt-backed picture onto the bottom of the dish.

Make It in a Flash

Haberdashery Box

Materials

Paper-covered box
4 shank buttons with woven leather tops
Hot glue
Ribbon
Mirror *(slightly smaller than the box lid)*
Clothing labels
Alphabet letter
Scrap paper
Tacky craft glue
Paper towels
Wide necktie *or other fabric to use for a cushion inside*
Cotton balls
Piece of cardboard *(slightly smaller than the
    bottom of the box)*

Tools

Craft knife
Hot glue gun
Scissors
Brush for glue

This little dresser box uses labels from vintage menswear as its decoration. Suit coats, shirts, and ties are all good sources. One of my local vintage shops gave me a stack of labels from damaged and unsellable merchandise. Church sales usually have the best prices on menswear, or hit the thrift store on a bag day. If you don't need the clothing, remove the labels and re-donate it.

'Everything's a Dollar' stores are a good place to find small paper-covered boxes. If need be, you can make your own. Use whatever size box you like. As reference, the box pictured is $4^{1}/_{2}$" x $3^{1}/_{2}$". The leather button feet are $^{1}/_{2}$". The mirror is 4" x 3". It's important that the mirror is mounted at least a $^{1}/_{4}$" in from all the edges so that it doesn't keep the lid from closing snugly. Cut yourself some slack and start with more ribbon than you probably need. The trimmed size of the ribbon for this box is 5".

Get on the good foot

1 Flip the box upside down. Poke the craft knife straight down through the bottom to make a cut in each corner, about a $1/2$" in from either side, and about a $1/4$" long. If you're using larger buttons, make the cuts further in from the edges.

2 Push the button shanks through the cuts until the button back is firmly against the bottom of the box.

Add a mirror & catch

3 Put a tiny dot of hot glue on one end of the ribbon and glue it to the inside of the box lid, about 2" up from the hinge and about 1" in from the edge.

4 Put a coil of hot glue on the back of the mirror, making sure there's some in the spot that will cover the ribbon. Try to avoid having any glue so close to the edges that it gushes out and makes a mess. Press the mirror in place.

5 Figure out the placement and length of the ribbon. Open the box lid. With one hand, hold the ribbon to the inside edge of the box base, about 2" out from the hinge. With the other hand, adjust the angle of the lid till it's relaxed and stays open without falling forward. Trim the ribbon to size and hot glue it in place.

Decorate!

6 Fuss with the labels. Clean off any loose threads or extra thicknesses of cloth behind them. Figure out how you want to arrange the labels and the alphabet letter on the box. You can cheat and trim the labels to fit your design, since fraying won't be an issue once you glue them down.

7 Using the scrap paper to keep your work area clean, brush glue on the back of the labels and then press them onto the box, using paper towels to blot up any excess.

8 Personalize the box with the alphabet letter. Hot glue it in place.

Make a cushion

9 Lay the fat end of the tie on your work area, lining-side up. Open it up, ripping some stitches if necessary. Put a pile of four or more cotton balls on it, followed by the piece of cardboard. Adjust the cotton balls so that you have enough to make a poofy little pad without it being so rotund that things will roll off.

10 Trim the fabric so that it's big enough to wrap around the back of the cardboard, folding the ends like you would wrap a gift. No need to pull it tight. A little excess fabric will fill in the gap between the cushion and the box. Hot glue the fabric edges.

11 Test to make sure the cushion fits inside the box well. Make any necessary adjustments.

12 From the inside of the box, drop a considerable pile of hot glue on each of the button shanks sticking through the bottom. Push the cushion down into place on top of them.

Glass
Menagerie

As an avid reuser, I'm delighted by the broad range of glass containers you can get for free at the grocery store, if you just buy what comes in them. Sadly, more and more glass containers are disappearing from the shelves, replaced by plastics that are neither very reusable nor very attractive. When the elegant amber glass Mrs. Buttersworth stepped down off the shelf for her flimsy plastic replacement, it was a dark day for retro crafters everywhere. Fortunately, some manufacturers still offer food in interesting glass jars, which means there will be crafters like me scrubbing out jars, peeling off labels, and storing them for future projects.

Masking Tape
Pleather Jar

Materials

Clean bottle *(interesting shape is a plus)*
Masking tape
Shoe polish in a can
Soft rag

This was a hippie-era dorm room fixture, right up there with the macramé plant holder and the Chianti bottle with candle drips. The method is frequently referred to in vintage publications as the "Leather Look." I'm not so easily fooled, hence the "Pleather."

I liked the lid on this bottle, so I left it on, but the truly classic "Leather Look" was a soda pop bottle transformed into a vase for dried flowers. It's an excellent watching-a-movie, talking-on-the-phone, I-wanna-be-sedated craft. It's as mindless as mindless can be, but the end result fetches plenty of compliments.

1 Round up every odd remnant of masking tape you can find; different tapes absorb the shoe polish differently, adding a fun "wild card" element to the finished piece.

2 Rip the tape into small pieces and put them on the bottle. Overlap them. Vary the size and orientation.

3 Keep ripping.

4 Keep ripping. It takes a while.

5 Cover the entire bottle. If you're making a vase, push some of the tape over the lip into the neck.

6 Rub shoe polish over the tape-covered bottle with the rag. It's like magic.

7 Polish it gently. The bottle pictured had one coat of brown polish. Mix it up by using more coats or other colors of polish.

8 Far out. Slip on a mood ring, light some patchouli incense, and dig out your copy of *Déjà Vu*. *(If you're a youngster, Google "Déjà Vu" with the initials "CSNY.")*

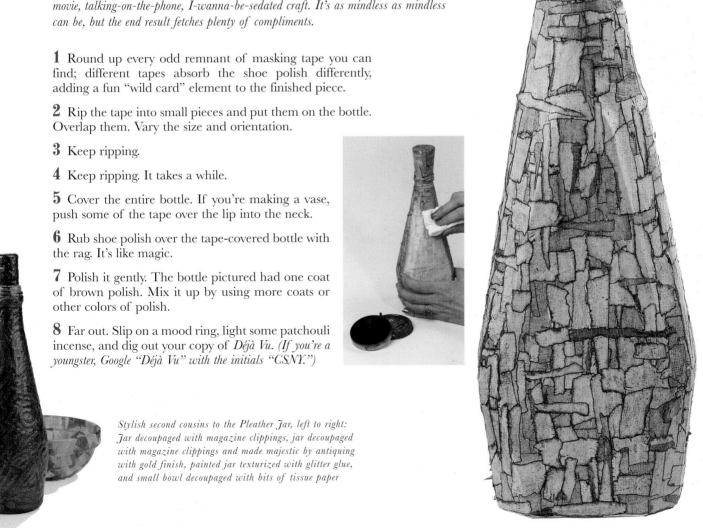

Stylish second cousins to the Pleather Jar, left to right: Jar decoupaged with magazine clippings, jar decoupaged with magazine clippings and made majestic by antiquing with gold finish, painted jar texturized with glitter glue, and small bowl decoupaged with bits of tissue paper

Sciencational Wind Chime

Materials

Science-themed or nature images
Single-strength glass:
    4 pieces cut 1" x 3"
    7 pieces cut $1^1/_2$" x $1^1/_2$"
Decoupage medium *(or self-leveling acrylic medium gel)*
Scrap of cardstock
Strip of cardstock, 17 x $1^1/_2$"
Glue stick
Colorful $^3/_4$" plastic tape
Hot glue
Paper towels
Thread
Aquarium sealant
8 prepared microscope slides
Sequins
Beads *(optional)*
Plastic ring

Tools

Craft knife
Straightedge
Brush
Scissors
Hot glue gun
Access to a sink, or a bowl of water
Sturdy needle

This tinkling tribute to Biology 101 uses image transfers to make light-catching translucent chimes. Look for science-themed and/or nature images in vintage textbooks, children's books, and periodicals—all easy finds at used bookstores. Color copy or scan them if you want to preserve the original. Prepared micro-scope slides are available new at science and education supply stores, and used at many places in the Trash Trifecta.

Prepare image transfers

Image transfer is an easy way to make your own decals from almost anything on paper printed with ink. The ink actually lifts off the paper and sinks into the medium.

1 Pick images to use behind each piece of glass. Use the glass pieces as templates to trim the images to size.

2 Brush a heavy coat of acrylic medium on each piece of glass.

3 Lay the trimmed images facedown in the wet medium on the glass. Use a scrap of cardstock to press the images smoothly against the glass and remove any air bubbles. Set aside to dry.

Make the top ring

4 Cut out fun science pictures to cover all but the last inch of the cardstock strip, which will be overlapped when the strip is glued together. The project pictured used old science textbook imagery cut into $1^1/2$" x $1^1/2$" pieces, and $1^1/2$" x 3" pieces. Glue stick them in place on the cardstock.

5 Cut a $1^1/2$" length of the $3/4$" plastic tape, and then cut it in half lengthwise, so that it's $1^1/2$"" x $3/8$". Press it on the strip in a space where two images meet, overlapping it onto each. Continue until all the seams between the images are covered.

6 Cut a piece of plastic tape a little longer than the strip. Cover the top $3/8$" with the tape, overlapping it over the images. Press the excess tape over the top of the strip and onto the back, smoothing out any wrinkles. Repeat on the bottom.

7 Flip the strip over and cover any exposed cardstock on the backside with plastic tape.

8 Put hot glue on the blank end of the strip, and press the other end onto it to form the top ring.

9 Cut a piece of plastic tape $2^1/2$" long, and cut it in half lengthwise. Center it over the seam where the two ends of the strip were joined, and press it in place, pushing the excess over the top and bottom edges onto the back.

Back to the transfers

10 Check to be sure the image transfers are dry. The acrylic medium should be crystal clear underneath the glass. If it's cloudy, the transfers aren't dry yet—you must have slapped that top ring together awfully fast. Give yourself a gold star for speediness, but wait till the transfers are completely dry before moving on to the next step.

11 Remove the paper from the back of the glass pieces by holding them under running water and gently rubbing the paper away. Rubbing too hard can make a hole in the transfer, so be gentle. I like to leave a little film of paper on the back for a more vibrant image. Taking more paper off makes the image more transparent. Lay the glass side down on paper towels to dry. (*If you're not happy with a transfer, scrape it off with a razor blade and start all over again.*)

Assemble the dangles

12 Cut 17 pieces of thread, each 24" long.

13 Put a small dot of silicone about $1/2$" from the top on the backside of the microscope slides and glass pieces. Put the end of a piece of thread into the silicone, and press a sequin on top of it to pin it down. A little silicone should come up through the hole in the center of the sequin. Put a bead in that. I used bugle beads because they're gaudy and iridescent like the bugs on my chimes. Set them aside to dry.

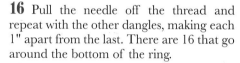

Hang 'em high

Description of hanging pattern:
  Diamond (2" from rim)
  Microscope slide (2½" from rim)
  Rectangle (4" from rim)
  Microscope slide (2½" from rim)
    (Repeat 3 more times)

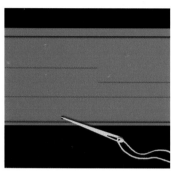

a. first stitch in back of the band

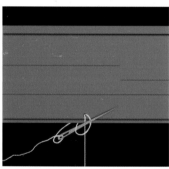

b. knotting the dangle

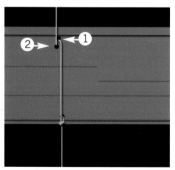

2 → **1**

c. securing thread at the top of the band

14 Thread a needle with the string from one of the dangles. Push it from the back of the ring to the front, about ⅛" above the bottom edge *(a)*. Adjust the length of the dangle. Knot the thread by pushing the needle back through the hole you just made, from the back to the front again, and then through the loop made by that stitch *(b)*. Pull thread tight to knot, being sure to keep the dangle the right length.

15 Without cutting the thread, pull it straight up the back of the ring and push the needle through the top of the ring from the back to the front, ⅛" from the top, directly above the knot you made below *(c1)*. The needle should be on the front now. Make a tiny stitch, about 1/16" down from where the needle came out, and push the needle to the back again *(c2, and photo below right)*.

16 Pull the needle off the thread and repeat with the other dangles, making each 1" apart from the last. There are 16 that go around the bottom of the ring.

17 There should be three dangles left to hang in the center of the chime. Arrange the first to hang just below the lowest dangles on the ring, the top of the next should be even with the bottom of the ring, and the last should be centered between those two.

18 Collect all the threads in one hand and hold them centered over the ring, about 6" above it. With the other hand, adjust the band and the strings till the band is level. This takes some futzing.

19 Wrap the strings around the plastic ring a couple of times, and then tie a tight knot to hold them in place.

20 Trim the ends about 1½" from the knot.

Sciencational! Give yourself a pile of gold stars.

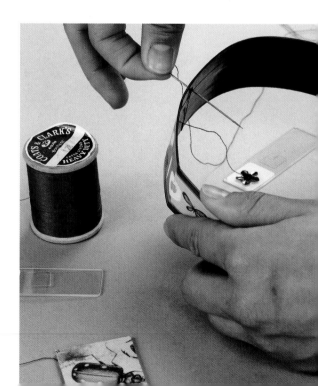

It Looks Like a Priceless Heirloom, But It's

Just a Memento

Materials

Plate
Convex glass that fits comfortably into the plate
Photograph
Cardboard
Masking tape
Antique gold paint *(acrylic will keep things speedy)*
Epoxy *(epoxy will keep things speedy as well)*
Plastic table knife
Trims: ribbon, flowers, buttons, etc.

Tools

Pencil
Scissors
Small paintbrush

Choose a plate that matches the era and the attitude of the photo you're using. Select a piece of convex glass that fits well inside the plate, leaving plenty of rim still showing. You can buy convex glass new from places that sell clock supplies. Old clocks are a great source of domed glass. Keep an eye out for them when you're junking. All the better if they're not working, but sometimes even when the clock still works, the junk dealer may sell you the clock and all for less than the price of the glass. Religious icons and dried flower arrangements from the 1970s are also good sources for domed glass.

Take the plate with you to the store to find exactly the right piece. Prices can vary wildly so do your homework first by calling ahead, or checking prices online.

1 Use the glass as a template to trim the photo and the cardboard to size.

2 Put the photo, facing up, on top of the cardboard, and put the glass over them both.

3 Tear off a piece of masking tape about a quarter of the circumference of the glass. Run it around the edge of the assembled photo and glass, with about $1/16$" overlapping onto the glass.

4 Press the tape down against the glass, allowing it to pleat to maintain an even curve. Flip the photo dome over. Smooth the tape out on the back of the cardboard. Continue placing and smoothing tape till the entire edge of the glass is sealed to the cardboard and photo.

5 Paint the top and side edges of the tape antique gold.

6 Use the plastic knife to mix epoxy directly on the center of the plate, keeping well within the area that will be covered by the photo dome.

7 Apply a thin, even coat of epoxy to the back of the cardboard, and immediately press down in the center of the plate.

8 Use epoxy to add trims.

These make great gifts because they're so easy to customize, and endlessly adaptable for all sorts of occasions. See page 173 for a children's gift suggestion. Include a plate stand or hanger.

Barnum + Baby Food
Jar Circus

These circus characters were designed to capture the quick-off-the-brush cartoon style of the early 1960s, maybe inspired by all the cereal boxes I stared at during my formative years.

Style-over-exactitude will give your teeny troupe a lively look, so cut the felt with a crisp imprecision.

Materials

Baby food jars, 1 tall and 4 medium
Spray paint, black and 2 colors
Cardstock, black and white
Tacky craft glue
Glitter pipe cleaners
Hot glue
Felt
Scrap of cardstock
Toothpicks
Red vinyl tape
Flat round sequins
Small artificial flowers
Candies, toys, or trinkets

Tools

Craft knife
Straightedge
Brush for glue
Wire cutters
Scissors
Hot glue gun

For the Ringmaster

Prepare the lid & base

1 Start with a tall jar. Spray paint the outside of the lid black.

2 Cut a strip of black cardstock 8½" x 2".

3 Brush a coat of craft glue on the front side of the strip, stopping about ½" from one end. Shake black glitter on it.

Details, details, Ringmaster

Use hot glue to attach details made from pipe cleaners. Remember to be kind to your scissors and snip the pipe cleaner with wire cutters. Unless otherwise noted, use craft glue to attach felt. Instead of trying to squeeze craft glue onto tiny bits of felt, squeeze it out onto a scrap of cardstock, and apply it to the felt with a toothpick. Keeping with the cartoon spirit, make no attempt to achieve symmetry with the facial features.

Ears: Snip two small pieces of pink pipe cleaner (about 1¾"), and roll into coils. Hot glue to tall skinny baby food jar.

Nose: Cut a triangle of pink felt. Snip the pointy tip off the end. Glue to the center of the jar. Cut a little brown felt trapezoid to go under it for a shadow. Cut two very small circles of black felt for nostrils and glue one to each side.

Eyes and brows: Cut two marquis-shaped pieces of white felt. (If you're not sure what marquis-shaped is, it's eye-shaped.) The pupils are black. Snip the brows willy-nilly. Remember, symmetry is not your friend.

Mouth and mustache: Cut two skinny, long triangles for the mustache, and glue them under the nose. Cut a scrap of red felt into a skinny little smile.

Hat: Screw the black lid on the jar. Cut a piece of black felt 4½" x 2". Hot glue it into a tube shape, then hot glue it to the center of the lid. Cut a small circle of black felt for the top of the hat and hot glue it in place. For a hatband, cut a piece of red vinyl tape and stick it around the base of the hat.

Assemble the base

4 Put hot glue on the end of the black cardstock strip without glitter, bring the other end around and press it down into the glue. Hold for a sec if you need to.

5 Give him a shirt. Cut a tall, skinny triangle (about $2^1/_2$" long) from white cardstock. Hot glue the back of it and put it on the top edge of the center front of the base (with seam in back).

6 Make his bow tie. Cut two little triangles out of two different colored flat sequins. Hot glue them to the shirt.

For the Critters

Prepare the lids & bases

1 Spray paint the outside of the lids. If you're making multiple critters, paint half one color and half the other for a nice, coordinated look.

2 For each base, cut a strip of white cardstock 1" x 8". (8" works for a standard baby food jar).

3 Brush a coat of craft glue on the front side of the strips, stopping about $1/_2$" from one end. Shake white and silver glitter on.

Details, details

Refer back to the note for Details, details Ringmaster for some general pointers. As a shortcut for making circles for the critter eyes, I used a rag to wipe the edge of a couple of marker caps clean, then pressed them down into the felt to make circular indentations I used as guides to cut around.

Tiger

Ears: Snip two small pieces of orange pipe cleaner (about $1^3/_4$" each), and roll into coils. Hot glue to baby food jar. Glue a tiny circle of gold felt to the center of each.

Nose and mouth: Cut a 1" circle of gold felt. Glue to jar. Cut a small triangle of red felt for the nose and glue to the circle. Cut a skinny black felt smile and glue below nose.

Eyes: Cut two small circles of white felt and two smaller circles of dark brown felt. Glue them to the jar above and to the sides of the nose.

Stripes: Cut eight skinny triangles in varying sizes. Glue two shorter ones between the eyes, and three on each side.

Zebra

Ears: Snip two $3^1/_2$" pieces of white pipe cleaner and bend each in half. For each piece, twist the ends together and bend up $1/_4$" to form a base. Screw a lid on and hot glue the ears on top of it. Cut two small diamonds out of pink felt. Glue to the center of each ear.

Nose and mouth: Cut a $3/_4$" circle of black felt. Glue to jar. Cut two tiny bits of pink felt to make nostrils, and glue to the circle. Cut a skinny red felt smile and glue below nose.

Eyes: Cut two small circles of white felt and two smaller circles of dark brown felt. Glue them to the jar above and to the sides of the nose.

Stripes: Cut eight skinny triangles in varying sizes. Cut six more really small triangles. Glue the smaller ones above the eyes, two of the others between the eyes, and three on each side.

Elephant

Ears: Cut two large petal shapes out of pink felt. Pinch the slightly pointy end together to make a small fold. Glue to each side of the jar.

Trunk: Cut a 2" x 3" piece of pink felt. Hot glue a piece of pink pipe cleaner, slightly shorter than 3", along one of the 3" edges. Roll into a long, uneven cylinder so that one end is about as wide as a pencil, and the other end is rolled loosely, with the felt barely meeting. To make a seam, put a little hot glue under the edge, from the skinny end to the middle, leaving the wide end unglued. With the seam on top, put a finger across the top of the felt, and bend the felt up and then down at the tip to look like a trunk. (The pipe cleaner glued inside allows you to shape it.) Put hot glue on the wide end, and position it in the center of the face.

Mouth: Cut a small circle of dark brown felt, and glue it under the trunk. Add a tiny white trapezoid for teeth.

Eyes: Cut two small circles of white felt and two smaller circles of dark brown felt. Glue them onto the jar above on either side of the trunk.

Bear

Ears: Snip two small pieces of brown pipe cleaner (about 1¾") each, and roll into coils. Hot glue to baby food jar. Glue a tiny circle of tan felt to the center of each.

Nose and mouth: Cut a 1" circle of tan felt. Glue to jar. Cut a small triangle of black felt for the nose, and glue to the circle. Cut a skinny red felt smile, and glue below nose.

Eyes: Cut two small circles of white felt and two smaller circles of dark brown felt. Glue them to the jar, above and to the sides of the nose.

Finish the lids & bases

4 Put a lid on any un-lidded critters.

5 To decorate a lid, trim the stem of a small artificial flower to 1" or so. Clip a small leaf (cut one from felt if you need to). Put a small spot of hot glue to one side on the top of the lid, put the end of the flower stem into it, and press the leaf on top to hold it down and cover the glue. Do as many as you want, but I don't like to leave anybody out of the fun.

6 For each critter's base, put hot glue on the end of the cardstock strip without glitter, bring the other end around, and press it down into the glue.

7 Cut two triangles out of felt for each critter, one in each of the colors you used to paint the jar lids. Try to make them a little lopsided and spontaneous looking. Hot glue them to the bases to form frisky bow ties.

8 Fill them up! I used wrapped candies in colors that coordinated with the critters, and orange marshmallow peanuts in the ringmaster. This troupe isn't easily washed, so stick with wrapped treats. (Toys, trinkets, and colored sand are two other options.) Because of the tiny embellishments, these are not toys for kids who still put things they shouldn't into their mouths.

9 Invent more characters for your circus, and be sure to email me pictures of them!
(suziemillions@charter.net)

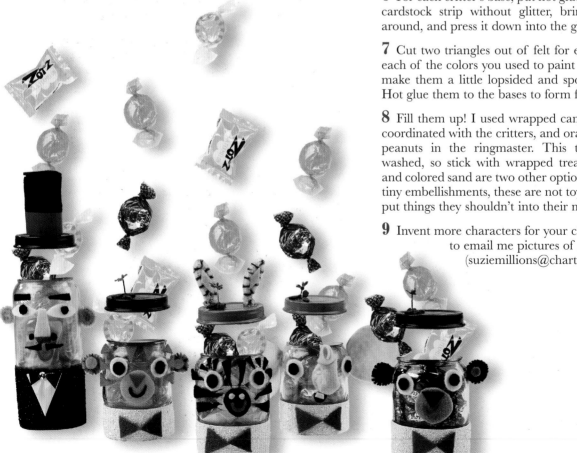

Among my Pseudo Souvenirs

Materials

Clear sheet protector

Clear glass ashtray

Vintage photo or magazine clipping

Self-adhesive felt, preferably dark green

Oil-base metallic gold paint

Fine aquarium gravel

Aquarium sealant

Tools

Marker that will write on plastic

Scissors

Brush

Box lid or bowl to put gravel in

Plastic table knife

Rag

Aquarium sealant in the small tube works really well for this project. Other adhesives labeled "crystal clear" will work, but they need to be thick enough to hold the gravel in place. Also, some "crystal clear" products are kidding themselves. If in doubt, test on the side of an old jar.

Get ready to rock

1 Make a template by laying the sheet protector on the back of the ashtray and tracing around the flat area where the image will go.

2 Cut out the template. Trace around it on the vintage photo or magazine clipping you've chosen, and cut it out.

3 On the backing paper for the felt, trace an outline that is about $1/4$" wider all the way around than the template. Cut out the felt.

4 Peel the backing paper off of the felt. Center the image on the adhesive side of the felt, leaving an even rim of the adhesive exposed. Press the felt-backed image onto the back of the ashtray, making sure all of the exposed adhesive makes contact with the glass.

5 Paint the top rim of the ashtray gold.

Rock out!

6 Pour a couple of inches of gravel into a bowl or box lid.

7 When the top rim of the ashtray is completely dry, run a bead of silicone around the outside. Use the plastic knife to spread it over the surface.

8 Hold the gluey ashtray with your thumb against the inside bottom and your fingers up against the felt on the outside bottom. Dip the ashtray into the bowl of rocks, pressing down, but not so firmly that it pushes the glue off the glass. Do your best to keep the silicone off the felt and your fingers.

9 Rotate the ashtray one turn, and press the other side into the rocks. Continue until it's rock-covered.

10 Shake off any excess. Touch up, if necessary. Use a rag to wipe off any rocks that have crept too far up onto the upper rim or down onto the felt. Wipe off any excess silicone.

variation

Paperweights are silly easy. Line up the paperweight over the image and trace around it. Trim the image $1/4$" or so smaller than your tracing *(to leave room for the felt to make contact with the glass)*. Hold the image over the felt, and cut the felt to be about $1/4$" larger than the image, all the way around. Peel the backing paper off the felt. Put the image in the center of the adhesive. Press the felt-backed image onto the back of the paperweight, and press to make sure the adhesive makes good contact with the glass. Secure some flighty papers.

Warming Up Exercise

Recipe for a Sweet Sweet Plate

LADY BIRD JOHNSONS PECAN PIE
Bake 350 deg.
1½ c pecans
1/3 c butter
3/4 c Brn. sugar
½ t salt
4 eggs
1 3/4 c corn sugar syrup
1 t vanilla

Spread nuts in bottom of pan on crust.
Cream butter,sugar,salt,add eggs,syrup,
vanilla.Pour over nuts,bake 45 min.

Materials

Vintage magazines, cookbooks, and
old recipe cards

Paper doilies

Clear plate

Paper towels

Decoupage medium

Backing (*use felt for a decorative plate, or tissue paper
and sealer for a plate you want to be able to hand wash*)

Tools

Scissors

Craft knife

Cookie sheet

Pencil

Drop cloth

Rag

Bowl of water

Brush for medium

Damp sponge

Brush for sealer

*Some examples of reverse decorated glass clockwise from top left:
customized decal ashtray for Rusty; pretty violet ashtray made
with a reverse decoupaged magazine clipping, backed by black
paint; and two examples of glass decorated in reverse with
postage stamps (a colorful retro craft favorite)*

Snip, snip, snip

1 Cut out gooey, gorgeous pictures of sugar-sprinkled delights. Clip some recipes, too. I'm especially fond of hand-scrawled notes next to recipes. Extinct advertising icons, dainty details clipped from paper doilies, and era-revealing recipe names ("Lady Bird Johnsons Pecan Pie") will give your plate the retro touch.

2 Plan your design. (Working on a cookie sheet will give you the luxury of moving the clippings easily if you need to.) Lay the clippings out and put the plate over them, upside down, to see how you're doing. Adjust until it's just so. Trace around the plate with pencil, and trim the clippings to size.

Set up & get messed up

3 Being organized going into this will reduce the stress of being up to your elbows in glue. Put a drop cloth down on your work surface. Set the bowl of water someplace above your elbow space so you don't tump it over. Lay a stack of paper towels to the side of that, and have the roll at the ready. Have a damp rag handy, too, to wipe your hands on when the need arises.

4 Pick up a clipping and drop it in the bowl of water. It will curl up at first and then flatten out. (This process of relaxing the paper will minimize wrinkling.)

5 Gently take the clipping out of the water when it flattens, and lay it on the pad of paper towels. Brush the entire front surface with the medium, and put it in place on the backside of the plate. Gently dab the back of it with the dampened sponge to push out any air bubbles and to set it firmly against the plate. The clippings are fragile when they're soggy, so handle them with care.

6 Repeat with the remaining clippings. Work with the front of the plate facing you, making sure there are no air bubbles or wrinkles showing on the face of the plate, and that the clippings are positioned how you want them to be. Turn it over now and then to check that things are flat and smooth on the back. You can overlap images all you like using this method.

7 When you're finished gluing on the images, brush an even coat of medium over the entire back of the plate, and leave it facedown to dry overnight.

Backing & finishing

If you plan to use the plate with food, it will need to be covered with tissue paper and then sealed. Felt is okay if you plan to hang the plate on the wall or only use it decoratively.

8 Put the plate upside down on the backing material, and trace around the outside edge. If there's a lot of paper overhanging the edge of the plate, trim it first with a craft knife.

9 Brush medium on the back of the plate. Smooth the backing over the medium, pressing out any wrinkles or air bubbles. Don't worry if the backing overlaps the plate edge at this point. Set the plate facedown to dry again overnight.

10 When it's completely dry, trim the excess backing from the rim with a craft knife. If you backed it with felt, skip ahead to step 12.

11 Apply a couple of coats of clear sealer to the back, allowing it to dry between coats per the directions for your sealer. Even with the sealer on it, hand wash only.

12 Clean up any errant glue or smudges on the surface of the plate. You're done! Go show it to somebody. Take them cookies on it for extra credit.

Whimsical
Whimsey Bottle

Materials

1950s' home and garden magazine
Black cardstock *(light enough to roll)*
White glue
1/8" x 1/8" balsa stick
1/32" x 4" x 36" balsa plank
Brown acrylic paint
Disposable cup for paint
1/4" cup of sand
Grass green hobby moss *(reindeer moss, or lichen; it should be soft and flexible, not crispy or dusty)*
2 very small artificial flowers
Hot glue
Game die
1 1/2" length of 1/4" x 3/8" balsa wood stick
Green acrylic paint to match the moss
Alphabet pasta
Scrap of cardstock
Toothpicks
1/2" glue dots
Bottle

Tools

Brush for glue
Pencil
Craft knife
Straightedge
Brush
Rag
Scissors
Hot glue gun
Small bowl

These are directions for making the bottle pictured. You can make one like it, or follow your own whimsey. See page 105 for even more whimsey bottle information, and pictures of actual pieces that may inspire you.

It looks daunting, but it's not very hard to make. Set aside a couple of hours, or if you plan on coming up with your own design, better set aside a day. The hardest part for me was convincing myself I could do it.

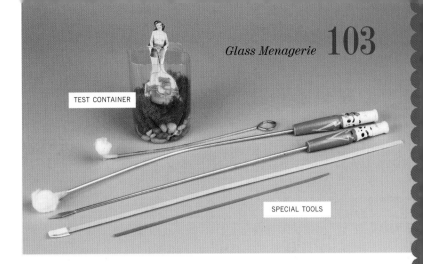

TEST CONTAINER

SPECIAL TOOLS

Special Prep Materials

Something to elevate the bottle on the work area

Materials to build special tools:
Four 18" lengths of Balsa sticks, $1/4$" x $3/8$"
Flexi-straw
Masking tape
2 paintbrushes
Tissue
Cardstock
Funnel with a long nose (*or a homemade paper funnel*)
A plastic container approximately the same size as the bottle
Craft saw

Prepare to be whimsical

1 It's nice to be able to see in the bottle at eye level while you work on it. Elevate it. I put a blender jar on my work desk, with a plate on top of that to set the bottle on.

2 This project requires some long-handled tools. To make extended handles for some of them, I used gigantically long (18"!) vintage barbecue skewers. Balsa sticks work well, too. They should be thick enough to be sturdy, but small enough to navigate the narrow space.

Flexible brush—Cut the elbow section out of a flexi-straw. Cut most of the handle off a cheap paintbrush, and push it into the elbow. Attach it to the elbow with masking tape, then tape the other end of the elbow to the extended handle.

Brush and buff—(*Used to clean off any specks on the glass inside the bottle.*) Pick a soft-bristled paintbrush that will fit through the bottleneck. Strap it onto an extension with masking tape. Wrap a couple of layers of tissue around the other end to make a soft pad. Tape them in place.

Paddle—(*The paddle helped me to arrange all the details inside the bottle.*) Cut a small piece of cardstock, around $5/8$" x 2". Fold it down to $5/8$" x 1", and attach it to the extension with a couple of drops of hot glue.

Funnel—(*If you plan on using any sort of substrata, like the sand in this bottle, you'll need a funnel to get it down into the bottle without making a mess. The funnel could also be used to direct small accessories to a specific place.*) You can buy a cheap, long-nosed funnel at an auto store. I rolled up a piece of cardstock and hot glued it together.

Poker—I used unembellished barbecue skewers and Balsa sticks to jab at stuff once it was inside the bottle.

3 Browse the grocery shelves for a clear plastic container that's close in size to your bottle. (*I found mine in the produce section, full of delicious juice.*) Clean it and cut it open with a craft saw. Use it to test your design ideas, and to adjust the size and quantity of what you plan on putting in the bottle.

Ready, set, go

4 Copy a happy mower and a ranch house from a vintage magazine. Mount them on black cardstock with white glue.

5 Put the $1/8$" x $1/8$" balsa stick in the bottle. Mark it at the place where it meets the lip. Take it out and trim it down to the mark.

6 Cut four strips, each 3" x $1/2$", from the $1/32$" balsa wood plank.

7 Water down a little brown acrylic paint in the disposable cup. Brush it on the balsa strips, front, back, and edges. Wipe off the excess with a rag. Brush and wipe the balsa stick you just trimmed, too. These will make your sign post.

Work in the test container

...until every piece of the design is made and put in place, and until these directions tell you to start working in the bottle.

8 Pour sand into the bottom of the test container.

9 Lay about 1" of moss on the sand. Hot glue a couple of tiny artificial flowers to it, along the front edge.

10 Add another piece of moss, about the size of an egg, on top of the moss already in the container.

11 Cut out the happy mower and the house.

12 Hot glue the die to the back of the mower, in the center of the bottom edge *(see photo above)*. Stand the mower up in the foreground of the test container, with the egg-shaped clump of moss behind her.

13 Hot glue the 1/4" edge of the 1 1/2" length of 1/4" x 3/8" balsa to the center back of the ranch house. Paint the top, front, and sides of the balsa strip green. Hot glue the house to the mound of moss in the back of the test container *(apply the glue to the bottom of the balsa strip)*.

14 Pour the alphabet pasta into a bowl. Pull out the letters to spell "WITH GOD AS MY WITNESS I'LL NEVER MOW AGAIN." Break a tiny curved piece off of a letter to make the apostrophe. Lay the letters out on the balsa planks as follows:

Plank 1 – WITH GOD AS

Plank 2 – MY WITNESS

Plank 3 – I'LL NEVER

Plank 4 – MOW AGAIN

Pour a little white glue on a scrap of card-stock, and apply it to the backs of the letters with toothpicks. Put them in place.

15 Put the balsa post for the signs in the center of the test container. Push down until it goes in as far as it can. Make a mark a little bit above the spot where the post meets the moss.

16 Press a glue dot in the center back of each of the four sign planks. With the bottom edge even with the mark you just made, press the bottom plank to the post. Add the other planks, about 1/2" apart. Tip them at different angles.

17 Assess your layout, and make any adjustments now.

You're ready to hit the bottle

Have your long-handled tools and whatever you plan on using to lift your bottle to eye level in place in your work space.

18 Lift the signpost, the happy mower, the ranch house, and then the moss out of the test container. *(I like to keep things together on a tray so nothing gets lost.)*

19 Give the bottle a last minute look-see to make sure it is absolutely spotless before you begin. Use your long-handled brush and buff tool to eliminate any specks or smudges.

20 Put the long funnel into the bottom of the bottle. Pour in the sand from the test container. Give the bottle a tiny wiggle to level it out.

21 Stuff the bottom layer of moss through the neck of the bottle, poking it in with your finger, saving the portion with the flowers till last. It's okay if it breaks off. Keep stuffing. Arrange it with one of the long-handled pokers so that the flowers are in the front of the bottle. Roll up the bump of moss with the house glued to it, and push it into the bottle. Use the long-handled poker to push down on the anchor strip behind the house to arrange it. It should be on top of the mound in the back of the bottle.

22 Gently roll the edges of the mower back until she's narrow enough to fit through the neck of the bottle. Do not crease her. You want her to relax and unroll after she clears the neck. Push her in. Arrange her with the long-handled paddle and a poker. Use a poker to push down firmly on the die mounted on her back to help place her. She should be front and center, and her lawn mower should appear to be chewing into that unruly lawn.

23 Gently push up on the ends of the signs so that they rotate on the post, staying attached, but lining up almost parallel to it. Guide the post through the bottle into the center of the bottle. Push down till it feels like it can't go any farther. Use the paddle to gently push the signs back into position.

24 Make like Edward Scissorhands, and use the long-handled brushes and tools to arrange things inside the bottle, and to clean up anything that needs tidying. Put a lid on it.

Whimsey Bottles

Whimsey bottles are a recognized form of folk art. Most of us have seen the ships in a bottle, but whimsey bottle makers put all kind of stuff in bottles—chairs, tassels, things with moving parts. A great resource to learn more about them is *Genius in a Bottle*, a very informative and richly illustrated book by Susan D. Jones.

I wanted to include a whimsey bottle in the book, but felt guilty about dabbling with something so many people have pursued with such focus and dedication. Then I had a slap-myself-on-the-head moment and recognized:

This is a "whimsey" bottle, not a "serious" bottle.

Although some whimsey bottle makers were informed by traditions handed down, there is no Whimsey Bottle School, and a lot of other folks probably taught themselves, too.

As for my rendition on page 102, I felt inspired to include a happy housewife in my bottle, accessorized by a ranch house and my personal motto, *"WITH GOD AS MY WITNESS, I'LL NEVER MOW AGAIN"*. (Home and garden magazines from the 1950s are rife with these merry mowers who seem only too eager to hit their little half acre in their strappiest sandals, behind a pre-self-propulsion, behemoth mower.)

I had the bright idea to put tiny little red ants in the bottom of my bottle that could only be seen when you looked from beneath. So I dropped in the ants, poured a little white glue over them, and planned to pour sand over that when it dried. The bottle broke out in a cold sweat and began to develop mold on the inside. New bottle. New ants. Squeezed some silicone in using an extension tube. The bottle fogged up, and the glue never set. More bottles, more glues, more mess. I ended up using a design that required no gluing inside the bottle. Not for lack of trying, I cannot recommend a glue to use inside the bottle.

A very special thank you to Susan D. Jones and Michael Williams for generously providing pictures of whimsey bottles from their collections. Bottles from Mr. Williams' collection include the Gosnell bottle pictured on page 12, and the Tassel Tree bottle, on this page, second from the right in the top row. The other whimsey bottle images in this book are from Ms. Jones' collection, except for the Elvis bottle on page 90, courtesy of the artist, Andrew T. Millon.

The Kitchen Sink

In addition to sometimes defying logic, some retro craft defies categorization. This section has a little of this, a little of that. A common thread running through all of these projects is this: They're not just fun and easy to make, they're *exceptionally* fun and easy.

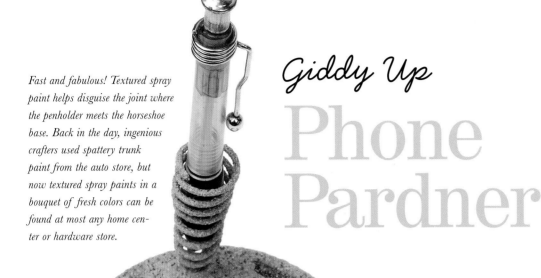

Giddy Up
Phone Pardner

Fast and fabulous! Textured spray paint helps disguise the joint where the penholder meets the horseshoe base. Back in the day, ingenious crafters used spattery trunk paint from the auto store, but now textured spray paints in a bouquet of fresh colors can be found at most any home center or hardware store.

Materials

Pen with personality
20" of 18-gauge steel wire
Epoxy
Small horseshoe
Textured spray paint
Scrap of cardstock
Toothpicks
2 small artificial flowers
8 flat back jewels

Tools

Wire cutters
Shot glass
Nail
Bottlecaps

Epoxy time

4 Set the shot glass inside the horseshoe to support the coil while the epoxy sets.

5 To help the epoxy adhere to the horseshoe, use the nail to scratch the surface at the center of the bend on the horseshoe, where the penholder will go.

6 Apply a generous puddle of epoxy to the area you just scratched on the horseshoe. Put the narrow end of the coil in the epoxy, and slide in the support to hold it up till it sets up.

After the epoxy is set

7 Gently angle the coil slightly toward the open end of the horseshoe.

8 Elevate the horseshoe on a few bottlecaps. Spray paint the horseshoe and coil, changing the angle of the spray can so that the underside and all the surfaces of the coil are covered.

After the spray paint dries

9 Bedazzle it. Mix a little epoxy on a piece of cardstock. Apply it with a toothpick to the artificial flowers and flat backed gems. Decorate the horseshoe base.

Make the pen holder

1 Wrap the wire around the pen. Holding the end of the wire even with the top of the pen, start wrapping about 3" from the pen point, and continue wrapping till you reach the point. Wrap a little loosely, but consistently, so that the coils are evenly spaced.

2 Pull the pen out and clip the coiled wire at the base and at the top, at a point just beyond where you began coiling.

3 Push the very topmost end of the coil down against the coil below it.

Saucy
Teacup
Cuties

Two-Minute Cutie

Dresser Valet

Materials

Cup and saucer
Acrylic paint for face
Rickrack
White glue
Block of plastic foam *(about 2" square)*
Epoxy that dries in 3-5 minutes
Plastic flowers
Toothpicks
Floral tape
Tulle
Button
Ribbon

Optional odds & ends:

Paintbrush and water
Decorative moss
More buttons, beads, bits of jewelry
Googly eyes
Pipe cleaners
Floral clay

Tools

Wire cutters
Scissors

Basic how—to

The basic directions follow, but be sure to read through the variations for ideas and inspiration for putting together these comely Cuties and putting them to work.

1 Paint a face on the cup.

2 Glue rickrack where you like on the cup and saucer, using white glue. The basic Cutie at far left has rickrack on the top of the cup and on the bottom rim of the upside-down saucer. Tiny rickrack on the cup handle always looks nice. Flip the saucer upside down, and glue rickrack to the lower rim using white glue. If it's an exceptionally pretty saucer, go ahead and leave it right side up.

3 Glue plastic foam in the bottom of the cup with epoxy.

4 Arrange the plastic flowers in the foam. Snip stems to size with wire cutters. If any of the flowers need additional sturdiness, wrap toothpicks to their stems using the floral tape.

5 Assemble a couple of puffs of tulle (see above right), and add them to the flowers to your taste.

6 When you're absolutely done fussing around with the inner cup decor, epoxy the cup to the saucer.

7 Use a toothpick to apply a little epoxy to the back of a button, and glue it center front on the saucer.

8 After the epoxy has set, tie some ribbon around the neck.

- *Try other facial options, including buttons, sequins, felt cutouts, features cut from magazines, googly eyes, and pipe cleaners.*
- *Tuck a pencil or penholder into artificial flowers. Use a pointy cake decorating point, a lipstick lid, or make your own out of cardstock.*
- *Add a holiday sentiment with a bakery pick or ornament.*

Making Tulle Puffs

Start with a length of tulle about 3" x 24". Holding an end firmly in one hand, push folds of tulle, about 1 inch-worth at a time, into that hand, rotating the collected tulle as you take new tulle in. Overlap a toothpick about a third of the way up the clump of tulle. Starting at the end of the toothpick overlapping the tulle, wrap the floral tape around it tightly several times until it feels sturdy, then continue wrapping toward the other end until the toothpick is covered. Tear the tape off the roll. Fluff the tulle. Vary the size of the puffs by using bigger or smaller sizes and amounts of tulle.

variations

Host/Hostess Gift: Substitute fresh flowers or a live plant for the plastic nosegay. Or fill the cup with a small bag of gourmet coffee and some biscotti.

Candy Caddy: Just fill 'er up! Or you can glue the plastic foam inside the cup but instead of plastic flowers, arrange a bouquet of lollipops with satiny bows tied around their sticks.

Bridal Shower Decor/Gift: Make a bride. Deck her out in white and pearls, and be sure to give her a tulle veil.

The Fast-as-a-Flash Two-Minute Cutie: Start with a lightweight plastic cup and saucer. For the features, use googly eyes and a small bit of pipe cleaner. Instead of glue, use floral clay to attach everything. Put a ball of floral clay into the bottom of the cup, lay a patch of decorative moss over the top, and push a couple of artificial flowers down into the clay. Use a small ball of clay to hold the cup to the saucer.

Dresser Valet: To catch combs, lose change, clippers, cuff links, and the like, glue the saucer right side up and leave the cup empty.

21 Brushstrokes to Loveliness
Teacup Cutie Cosmetology
Practice making quick, single strokes on a piece of paper!

1 TOP LEFT EYE	2 TOP RIGHT EYE	3 BOTTOM L EYE	4 BOTTOM R EYE
5 LEFT BROW	6 RIGHT BROW	7 LEFT LID	8 RIGHTLID
9 LEFT IRIS	10 RIGHT IRIS	11 LEFT PUPIL	12 RIGHT PUPIL	13 NOSE	14 TOP OF LIPS
15 FILL UPPER LIP	16 BOTTOM LIP	17 FILL B. LIP	18 WHITE L EYE	19 WHITE R EYE	20 21 HILITES ON LIPS

Sparklific
Plaster
Plaques

Materials

3 pictures copied from magazines, etc.
Petroleum jelly
Paper towels
2 to 3 glass Christmas ball ornaments that are
    broken, or that you're willing to break
Sturdy envelope
Plaster
Hairpin, wire loop, or hanger of some sort

Tools

Scissors
1 to 3 plastic kitchen storage container lids
Cookie sheet or tray
Hammer
Small plastic bucket
Paint stirrer
Knife (optional)

*Don't get flummoxed by the wealth of choices there are for
plaster. Plaster, or Plaster of Paris, is powdered gypsum;
and although the powder-to-water ratio may vary, it doesn't
make much difference which mutation you use when making
small, solid castings like these.*

Prepare to get plastered

1 Start with three images that look good together or create a theme. I went for station wagons. Trim them from their backgrounds.

2 Use a paper towel to rub petroleum jelly over every bit of the inside of the storage container lids. *I only had one container, so I made one plaque at a time.*

3 Put the lid(s) on a cookie sheet or tray. That makes it easy to move them if you need to, and catches any spills.

4 Lay the image facedown in the greased container lid.

5 Drop a couple of broken (or soon-to-be-broken) glass Christmas ball ornaments in the sturdy envelope. Pound with a hammer.

6 Sprinkle some ornament bits around the edges of the lid.

Cast off

7 Mix a small batch of plaster according to the directions on the package.

8 Slowly pour the plaster into the storage container lids. Fill close to the top. It doesn't expand, but if you fill the lids too high, you'll get a "muffin top" bulge.

9 After the plaster sits for a spell, add a hairpin, a loop of wire, or hanger of your choice to the center back of the plaque. *(It needs to set up a little, but not so much that it's too hard to add the hanger.)*

10 Let the bucket sit. Later when the plaster hardens, you can pour off the water, flex the bucket, and pop out the plaster. Never, ever, ever, pour plaster down a drain. Never. Ever.

When it's dry

11 Plaster is gray when it's wet, white when it's dry. After the casting looks more white then gray, carefully flex the lid, and the plaque should pop right out.

12 You can use a sharp knife to shave down any ridges or excess on the rim. I prefer not to fuss. Adjust the angle of the hangers on the back if needed.

Here is everything useful I can think to tell you about plaster:

Use cold water to keep it from setting up too quickly.

Put the water in a bucket first, then add the plaster on top of it. Always put the water in first.

Let the plaster absorb the water for a bit, then mix with a paint stirrer, gently.

Mix slowly, to keep air bubbles out, but don't mix for too long; it will start to set up on you.

The mixture should be smooth, and more like heavy cream than pudding.

After mixing, tap the bucket a couple of times to release air bubbles.

The Unmitigated Plaster Disaster

Here is everything useful I can tell you to **_not_** do when working with plaster:

a. *Don't use an inflexible object as a mold; your casting will be permanently bonded to it.*

b. *Don't use an image with printing on the back; the printing will show through.*

c. *Don't tint plaster with food coloring if you're using paper imagery in the casting; the tint will bleed into the image.*

d. *Grandma may have made plaster plaques in paper plates, but I'm guessing that, like her shoes and the fenders on her car, paper plates were sturdier back then. My paper plate castings buckled and spilled plaster all over the place.*

miscellaneous bad ideas

Cocktail Time
Frame Tray

Materials

Vintage magazines
Tray *(or something for sorting clippings)*
Decoupage medium
Sturdy wooden frame
Paper towels
Heavy backing *(same size as glass)*
Mirror *(same size as glass)*
Vintage bar recipe pamphlets
Clear acetate
Glue dots
Glass *(to fit frame)*
Framing push points
4 small self-adhesive rubber feet
2 drawer pulls
Choose pulls that can be screwed in from the front, and not from behind

Tools

Scissors
Paintbrush for decoupage medium
Flat-head screwdriver
Marker
Drill *(small hand drill, craft drill, or real deal)*
Screwdriver

Frame trays were a favorite shop project—a wooden frame, plus two drawer pulls, plus a nice picture, equaled a B+. This one would have earned an A+, dressed up in a geometric crazy quilt of vintage liquor ads and with a retro-spectacular reflective base.

I don't know if there's a name for this type of frame—dime-a-dozen might be appropriate. They were in vogue when Early American was the home decor de jour. This particular frame has nice corner details, but this general style is well represented wherever pre-owned home accessories are found, and it makes a very nice tray.

Rip it up

If you don't have a stack of vintage magazines, you may have to buy a couple. Ladies' magazines were not so big on the liquor ads. Look for Esquire, Holiday, Life—each of them had its share of advertisers from the spirits industry.

1 Settle down with a stack of vintage magazines. Look for liquor ads or other pages with photographs of barware, frosty drinks, people imbibing, or anything that conjures up cocktails for you. If it would break your heart to tear them up, copy or scan the images. Personally, I rip them out.

2 Get snippy. Cut the ads into small, straight-sided pieces: squares, triangles and rectangles. Go all op-art—cut indecipherable glimpses of lettering, logos, backgrounds, etc.

3 Keep your clippings sorted into broad categories. I like to use a multi-compartment cafeteria tray to stack them in. You'll have some truly spectacular clippings and lots of filler-type things. My clippings were sorted into piles: with lettering, close-ups of frosty drinks, with woodsy backgrounds, with blue skies, etc. Having them sorted makes it easier to keep the imagery balanced.

Glue it up

4 Decoupage the frame. Brush glue on the backs of the clippings. Let them curl and then relax a little. Smooth them on. Have lots of paper towels handy to dab the pieces down and to mop up the excess glue. Jump around from one part of the frame to another as you place the clippings so that the imagery is balanced. Cover the face and the outer edges. Don't use your spectacular pieces right away. Odds are they'll get covered up as the space starts to fill in. Save them for the icing.

Lay out the bottom panel

The first layer is a sheet of glass, the next is imagery, the next is a mirror, the next is a heavy backing material.

5 Lay the backing material facedown, with the mirror faceup on top of it *(I cut a panel from an old game board for the backing material. It was sturdy and water resistant.)*

6 Color copy or scan and print pages from vintage drink recipe books onto clear acetate. Arrange them on the mirror. Trim overlaps, or leave some that are visually interesting to you. Tack them all in place with small glue dots here and there.

7 Lay the glass down on top of it all. Set it aside for now.

Seal

8 Brush one or two coats of decoupage medium on the decorated part of the frame to give it a waterproof finish.

The backstory

9 When the frame is absolutely dry, flip it over and put in the assembled bottom panel. Use a flat-head screwdriver to install push points. Make sure there is one on each side of every corner and every 3" or so along the sides.

10 Press on the rubber feet.

11 Line up the drawer pulls in the center of each end. Mark where the screws should go. Use a drill to make guide holes. Screw the pulls in place. Stylish!

Now load that thing up with liquor, and pour yourself a neat one.

Happy Go Plucky
Bottle Buddies

Materials

Plastic foam ball
Hot glue
Bottle
Craft trims *(see list in step 3)*
Tacky craft glue
Glue dots

Tools

Steak knife
Hot glue gun
Wire cutters
Scissors

A steak knife is a good tool for cutting and carving plastic foam.

1 Choose a way to attach the head:

- *Quick and easy*: Shave a little slice off the ball, and use hot glue to attach it to the lid.

- *For open bottles that don't have a lid*: Carve a hole in the bottom of the foam ball so it can slide over the bottle neck.

2 Wrap pipe cleaners around the top of the bottleneck to make arms. Wrap little props at the ends of these.

3 Create eyes, ears, nose, and details from felt, sequins, beads, googly eyes, pipe cleaners, colored toothpicks, colored paper clips, buttons, glass head straight pins, pom-poms, pom-pom trim, rickrack, and anything else in your arsenal of craft geegaws.

4 Attach the details with tacky craft glue or glue dots. Use straight pins to attach sequins, and to hold felt and other materials in place until the glue dries. Pipe cleaners may not require glue; push the ends directly into the foam and hope for the best.

variations

Drinking Buddies: Alcohol! Googly eyes! Alcohol! Googly eyes! The irresistible sideways glance and bobbling outstretched arms of the Drinking Buddy will win hearts and mend fences wherever needed. Pictured on mini bottles, but why not scale it up for a googly gallon?

Well-coiffed Buddy (pictured above left): Start with a vintage satin Christmas ball made with a plastic foam ball core (most contemporary satin balls are made with hard plastic cores). Snip through all the "satin" threads at the base of the ball to release the satin thread covering. The satin can slide off very easily until you add a few drops of white glue under the threads on the top of the ball. After the glue dries, style her satin "wig." Snip some bangs. Tie up a couple of pigtails with curling ribbon. Pin in a couple of sequin star eyes, add a glass head pin nose, and a red sequin smile.

Just the Prescription
Pill Bottle Shrine

It's a Small, Small World

actual size

Ridiculously tiny, and quick and easy, this itty-bitty shrine is 1" tall. The container is a plastic vial from a bead store. The scene includes a figure snapped off the top of a cocktail pick, and a slim sprig of frosty winter foliage that fills out the background, all sitting on a tiny plastic foam ball cut in half, brushed with tacky craft glue, and sprinkled with iridescent glitter. For simulated snowfall, a couple of even tinier white foam balls plucked from an artificial evergreen spray were strung on white thread and looped through a hole on a white button. The needle was brought back down through another hole, then a couple more foam balls added, then the button was glued in place on top. A white sequin glued to the very top covers the thread and keeps the dangles balanced.

The Holiday Classic

Finding holiday figurines is like finding gummy, indiscernible objects in fruitcake—the thrift world is littered with little wooden ornaments, tiny plastic deer, and choruses of singing angels. Apply sequins or glitter to half of a foam ball, and plant a frosty pine branch. Cover the ugly lid with a bit of gaudy sewing trim. Finish it off with a crescendo of glue gunnery, layering tinsel garland, bits of Christmas light reflectors, plastic holly garland, and a loop of gold elastic, to hang it on the tree.

Four Seasons with Sushi Grass

I wanted these shrines to be on the big side, so I built them in the clear plastic canisters that colored toothpicks come in. Pill bottles work well, too; I just didn't have any pharmaceuticals in the cupboard. These containers are 3" high. The wooden disks are 2½". The foam balls were 1½". These work as a set because they all share the same basic elements, each tailored for the season that shrine represents.

Pert + Pensive
Plastic Flower Pixie

Materials

Bumpy green pipe cleaner
Plastic flower without stem
4" green pipe cleaner
Hot glue
Wooden face bead *(paint a plain bead if you want or need to)*
Bit of curly doll hair
Flower center to use as a crown
Bouquet of small flowers
4" sparkly pipe cleaner
2 pieces of plastic foliage for wings
Feather
White glue
Glitter

Tools

Wire cutters
Hot glue gun
Brush for glue

Hot glue melts most plastic flowers, so learn to regulate that to your advantage. Target where you want to put it, and use enough to melt a little of the flower to form a good bond with whatever you're gluing on. Avoid using so much that your bloom disintegrates. When attaching airy bits of plastic flower foliage or details, put the glue on what you're going to put the airy little detail on, and not on the airy little thing itself. Hot glue it directly, and it will probably wilt and melt, possibly on your fingers. Ow! Dual melt or cold melt guns are a little gentler, but you're still risking a meltdown.

Make her arms & legs

1 Cut the bumpy pipe cleaner in half.

2 Bend each half in half again. One will be the arms, and one will be the legs. On both, the end with the bend is the base.

Assemble the body

3 The plastic flower forms the body of your pixie, but not all plastic flowers are made alike. What follows are first the general directions for assembly, and then some tips to help you deal with likely variables.

This pixie wears her bloom upside down, as a skirt. Remove anything that might block the arms and legs from going through the center of the bloom.

Christmas Pixie

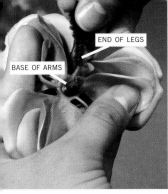

END OF LEGS
BASE OF ARMS

PHOTO 1

PHOTO 2

Push the base of the arms through the calyx (the tulip-shaped green cup at the base of the bloom), from the stem side to the bloom side. To interlock the arms and legs, on the bloom side, hook the legs through the base of the arms *(photo 1)*. Pull the legs through until the base of the arms is centered between them *(photo 2)*. Pull on the arms from the stem side, to bring the base of the legs up into the bloom.

Add the neck by pushing the 4" green pipe cleaner through the calyx and twisting the end of it over the joint where the arms and legs meet.

Add hot glue to the cup of the calyx and push the base of the bloom into it, pinning in the bases of the arms, legs, and neck.

Time to punt:

- *Sometimes there isn't a calyx. You can steal one off another flower, or make one out of felt.*

- *Sometimes the only thing that holds the entire bloom together is a piece stuck in the middle that you just pulled out to get the legs through. If your flower comes apart, put a little dab of hot glue in each layer, and stick it back together.*

- *If the arms and legs can't meet in the center, wrap the end of the neck around the end of the arms and glue that to the base of the flower. Use hot glue to anchor the base of the legs as deeply as you can in the center of the bloom.*

- *Bottom line, find something to glue the base of the neck, arms, and legs to.*

Get her head on straight

4 Check the length of the neck by slipping the face bead over it. Trim if necessary, leaving enough to put a loop at the end to make the face bead fit more tighty. Put a little hot glue in the bead, and put it on the neck.

5 Glue a curl of hair on top of her head. Use the center from a flower to make a crown, and glue it on top of her head.

Embellish

6 Put a tiny dot of hot glue onto the stems of the bouquet, and wrap the end of one of her arms around it.

7 Make a hanger by loosely bending the 4" sparkly pipe cleaner in half and twisting the ends together. In the center of her back, insert hot glue between the bloom and calyx. Stick the twisted end of the hanger into the glue, and hold it a sec until secure. Bend it up so the loop is on the top.

8 Put a bit of hot glue on her back, and put in wings made from plastic foliage. Put a feather in the glue before it dries.

Over embellish

9 Brush slippers on her feet with white glue. Dip into glitter and shake excess off.

10 Brush white glue on the edges of her petals, bouquet, and anywhere else you'd like to give her some bling. Shake glitter on, and shake the excess off.

11 Hang her up by the pipe cleaner hanger till the glue dries. Pose her by bending her arms and legs.

variations

Bundle of Joy (baby shower/new baby): Choose a pastel plastic bloom. Instead of a bouquet, give the pixie a swaddled baby to hold. To make the baby, paint a small bead flesh color. Add teeny tiny blue dots for eyes, plus a teeny tiny red dot for a mouth. Brush a hint of pink on the cheeks. Glue a bitsy wisp of hair to the top of the head. Turn a small square of white felt sideways to make a diamond. Fold the sides in and bottom up to make a baby burrito. Hot glue in place. Add the tiny baby face, and hot glue it in place. Wrap the arms around tightly. Babies like to be snug.

Christmas Pixie: Start with a red or white bloom. Trim her skirt and sleeves with sparkly tinsel garland. For wings, use plastic holly leaves frosted with chunky white glitter. Give her a tiny gift to hold. Frame her face with the ermine-like end of a white feather.

Bundle of Joy

The Match Game

Once upon a time—a smoky, carcinogenic time—-if a patron slid a cigarette out of the pack, a waiter would glide in and snap open a lighter. Folks were smoking up a storm. Every business establishment had a bowl brimming with colorful, custom-imprinted, complimentary matchbooks next to the register. Matchbook salespeople were living large.

That abundance made for common retro craft material. Crafters used matchbook covers to decoupage in colorful patchwork, matchboxes to build things, and matchsticks to encrust or construct. Matches may not be ubiquitous, or as free, as they used to be, but they're still a relatively inexpensive, and very versatile, crafting material.

Adhesives for Matchsticks

Tacky craft glue is your all around go-to adhesive to use when working with matchsticks. Some vintage publications recommend rubber cement. It's so easy to work with—I was really pulling for it—but finished pieces made with it are noticeably more fragile.

Quick as a wink

Matchbook Notebooks

How to Burn Matches

Geeze Louise, am I really going to tell you how to burn wooden matchsticks. Yep—just a couple of pointers that will make things easier for you.

If you're going to burn a lot of matches in one sitting, light a candle. Hold more than one match in the flame to save time. Burning up to four at a time is manageable; more is not.

To make uniform matchsticks, after you strike the matches, let them burn for a couple of seconds. If they don't burn long enough, some of the coating remains on the head, making them thicker. If they burn too long, they'll be shorter, and possibly too spindly to use.

Use a rag to wipe off the ashy ends into an ashtray or other nonflammable receptacle.

Store the matchsticks with the burnt ends facing the same direction. When you're gluing a big mess of them on something, you'll be glad you did.

Burn the matchsticks before you use them!

Burn Baby Burn

I really like the look of unburned, bright red match heads on some vintage projects, but couldn't figure out a way to defuse them. I conducted numerous experiments in the craft lab, coating the match heads with all kinds of stuff, but every attempt went up in smoke.

Pull those great-looking old matchbooks out of the big glass jar, and press them into duty as super-swell mini note pads. Measure the back panel of the matchbook. Cut plain paper 1/8" smaller than that measurement. Two common sizes are:

Large book (2" x 1⅞")........*note paper 1⅞" x 1¾"*

Small book (1⅞" x 1½") ...*note paper 1¾" x 1⅜"*

Cut 24 sheets for each pad. Clip a fun vintage image to use for the front sheet. If it isn't printed on sturdy paper, glue stick some decorative paper behind it. The inside covers of some matchbooks have great graphics. If yours doesn't, glue stick some decorative paper to it.

With a staple remover or a small screwdriver, take out the small staple on the front of the matchbook that holds in the match strip. Get rid of whatever bits of the strip remain. Use a punch that makes a small hole (1/8" or so) to make a hole about 1/4" down from the top edge, and in the center of the short front panel of the matchbook where the staple was.

Punch a corresponding hole in the notepaper, centered along and 1/4" up from the bottom edge. Put a small brad through the front of the matchbook and the notepad. Press the ends flat on the last sheet of notepaper.

Carry these in pocket or purse. When you use it, flip the pad out and use the paper from the back to the front, preserving the first sheet with the vintage picture.

Make One For Your Daddy

Matchstick Desk Caddy

Materials

Clear plastic sheet protector
Cardboard pencil box, or other sturdy, lidded box
2 small containers
Notepad
Spray paint
Tacky craft glue
A lot of wooden matches *(prepared as directed on page 121; this design uses 800+)*
Scrap paper
Amber varnish
4 bottlecaps

Tools

Marker that works on plastic
Ruler
Craft knife
Pencil
Brush for glue
Sturdy utility scissors
Brush for varnish

I like to use restaurant receipt pads for phone messages. After the original message is long lost, there's still a carbon copy back-up. This handsome organizer holds a pad, writing implements, and plastic flowers. You can customize yours to hold whatever you like to have handy. This box uses containers that are the same height as the box, a plastic film canister, and a plastic container that colored toothpicks came in. You can use more shallow containers if they have a rim that can support them; rimmed jar lids are great for making shallow wells for paperclips and the like.

Warning: *Matchsticks are contagious. The handsomeness of this box just might inspire you to start covering your other desk accoutrements. A candy gram goes to the first person to send me a picture of their computer monitor or CPU covered in matchsticks. (If it's company property, chances are you'll be sharing those candies with your former coworkers.)*

People get ready

1 Make templates to use later by making a tracing on the sheet protector of the long side and the short side of the pencil box. Cut them out and put aside.

Mark & make the openings

2 Flip the box upside down so that the bottom of the box is on top. If you're using a pencil box with a hinged lid, put the hinged side in front—it has a smoother profile than the side with the front edge of the lid.

3 Figure out where you want to put the containers on the top of the box. Set them there with the opening side down on the top of the box, and trace around them.

4 Measure the width and thickness of your notepad and mark a slot for it to stand in, about $3/8$" wider and $1/8$" deeper than the pad. If you make the hole too deep, the pad will slouch instead of standing up nicely. For this Guest Check pad, the opening is $3^3/4$" x $1/2$".

5 Use the craft knife to cut out the marked openings.

More prep

For the interior, pick any color that speaks to you. This box has rich brown, but lately turquoise is putting a bug in my ear.

6 Spray paint:

- the edges of the openings you just cut out
- the inside bottom panel *(the underside of what was the lid)*
- the interior of the two containers.

7 Put the containers in place in the box.

Make designs

Because the openings on your box may be different from mine, you'll have to make your own design for the top of the box. I used the classic matchstick cross pattern (see photo in chart below) as a launching point, and freestyled it beyond that. Take a closer look at the vintage pieces on page 120 for additional reference.

8 Decide on a pattern for the top of the box. *(Sketch it out if you'd like.)*

Git to stickin'

9 Paint a thick coat of tacky craft glue on what is now the top panel of the box.

Matchstick Patterns

Simple Zigzag

(as done on the box shown; inspired by this cross)

Nine matches down, one match in the center, then nine matches up. On the downstroke, the burned head of each successive match is just below the last. On the upstroke, each head is just above the last. This 19-match pattern is repeated all the way across the panel. Begin the first match even with the upper left hand corner of the paper and continue all the way across. Begin the second row on the far left edge, fitting the matches in tightly against the ones in the first row. Don't mind the little V-shaped gaps along the top and bottom edges; those will be filled in later.

10 Frame the opening for the notepad with a single-file line of matches *(see photo at right)*.

11 Following your design, press matches in place on top of the box. Add all the whole matches first, then trim and place the rest. *(To trim matches, hold the match where you would like to position it, mark the cut line with a pencil, and use sturdy scissors or a large nail clipper to cut it to size.)* If the glue begins to dry, recoat where necessary.

Side stickin'

To keep the pattern even from one panel to the next, the matches are glued to paper panels. After the panels are covered with matches, the clear acetate templates are positioned over them to mark the matches for trimming. The clear templates allow you to see the match pattern below so that you can choose how you would like to crop the panels (the pattern is centered on mine.) The panels are cut to size with scissors, then mounted on the box.

12 For the sides and end panels of the box, cut panels of paper 2" longer and 2" taller than the actual dimensions.

13 Work on one panel at a time. Brush a thick coat of craft glue on the paper and make the Simple Zigzag pattern *(described in the chart at lower left)*.

14 For each of the two side panels, lay the clear template of the box side over the match-covered panel. Use a pencil to trace around the template directly onto the matches. Trim to size with sturdy scissors, clipping through the matches and paper. Apply craft glue to the small V-shaped gaps on the edges of the panel, and fill in with matches. Trim again.

15 Repeat with the end panels.

16 Glue the completed panels in place. *The tops of the panels should be even with the top surface of the box, not the matches on top of it. A line of matches will be added next to cover all the match ends.*

Trim & varnish

17 Brush craft glue on the upper edge of the side panels. Trim these edges with a single-file line of matches to hide all the match ends *(see photo above right)*.

18 Finish with two coats of amber varnish. Wait between coats, per the directions on the varnish. *When you varnish, elevate the box with a bottlecap under each corner to keep it from adhering to whatever you have underneath it.*

Summer Camp Classic

Matchstick Frame

Frame Size Calculator

When framing, precise fits make for a more difficult time. You want an image that is slightly larger than the frame opening, but one in which you won't miss the little bit around the edges that the frame will cover. This formula makes the frame opening $\frac{1}{4}$" smaller than the image you want to display, giving you $\frac{1}{8}$" of wiggle room all the way around. And in case it makes a difference when you select an image, the matchsticks extend $\frac{1}{4}$" beyond the frame opening, so $\frac{1}{4}$" of the image exposed by the opening is overlapped by the matches.

The easy way to do this is to make a frame first, then find a picture to put in it. To customize the frame to fit a specific image, you can use the formula below.

The Formula

Frame Opening = *Image Size* minus $\frac{1}{4}$"
Frame Face = *Length of Match* minus $\frac{1}{2}$"
Size of Frame = *Frame Opening* + (*Frame Face* x 2)

The frame pictured above is $8\frac{3}{4}$" x $6\frac{3}{4}$", with a $6\frac{1}{4}$ x $4\frac{1}{4}$ opening. The frame face is $1\frac{1}{4}$". The matches used were $1\frac{3}{4}$".

Materials

Corrugated cardboard
Plain cardboard
Tacky craft glue
Burned matchsticks *(prepared following the directions on page 119)*
Business card *(any)*
Hot glue
Double-sided tape
Photograph
Embellishment for corners *(aquarium gravel, glitter, small shells)*
Amber varnish
4 bottlecaps
Sheet protector *(or other clear plastic for opening; optional)*
Self-adhesive loop-and-eye tape dots *(optional)*

Tools

Ruler
Pencil
Craft knife
Brush for glue
Hole punch
Hot glue gun
Sturdy utility scissors
Brush for varnish

A cutting mat is very useful for this project.

This matchstick frame could be made with a sturdier material for the base, but I really like the simplicity of using cardboard. The Frame Size Calculator (see previous page) let's you choose the size of the image and create a frame to fit, but use a photo that is 5" x 7" or smaller. If it's larger, the strength and suitability of cardboard will become issues. If you're in a hurry, skip ahead to the Flash Fire Fast variation (on the next page).

Make frame base

1 Figure out your frame size using the *Frame Size Calculator*.

2 Use a ruler to draw the frame on corrugated cardboard. Cut out the frame and frame opening with a craft knife.

Make corner pieces

3 Cut four squares out of plain cardboard for corner pieces. The sides of the squares should be $1/4$" shorter than a matchstick. *(My matchsticks were $1^3/4$" long so my corner squares were $1^1/2$" square.)*

4 Draw a line diagonally across each corner piece.

5 Brush an even layer of tacky craft glue on a corner piece. With the upper end of the diagonal line in the upper left-hand corner, put a matchstick on that line, with the burned end to the left, hanging $1/4$" over the edge. Continue adding matches, keeping a straight line on the top and left edge. *Don't worry about the gap in the lower right-hand corner, or the overlap on the bottom and right. We'll come back to that.*

6 Repeat with the other corners. Set aside to dry.

Assemble the back panel

7 Make a tracing of the frame and opening on plain cardboard. Cut out the frame to make a back panel, but don't cut out the opening.

8 To mark where the hanger should go on the back panel, flip the back panel over so the tracing of the opening is on the side lying down. Measure its width, and make a mark about 1" down from the top edge and centered exactly from side to side.

9 Make a hanger. Fold the business card in half. Punch a hole about $1/2$" down from the fold. Hot glue the open end of the card shut. With the punched end up, line up the hole in the card so that you can see the mark you just made. Add some hot glue to the base of the card, and press it in place.

10 Flip the panel over. Put a strip of double-sided tape along the top edge on the back of the picture. Line it up over the opening space indicated, and press it in place.

Install corners

Steps 7 to 10 were designed to give the corner pieces some drying time (20 minutes or so). Once dry, continue on.

11 On each corner piece, use sturdy scissors to trim the matches overhanging on the bottom and right side. Make them even with the edge of the cardboard.

12 One corner at a time, put a puddle of hot glue in the center of the corner area on the frame base, and place a corner piece in it, burned ends facing out. The cardboard edge of the outer corner of the corner piece should line up with the outer corner of the frame base. The inside corner overlaps the frame opening. Flip the frame over, and make sure each corner is properly aligned before moving on to the next corner.

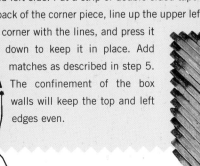

Suzie Do

To make the corners straight and even, build a jig in a small, shallow box (I use a gelatin box). Mark lines $1/4$" from the top and left side. Put a strip of double-sided tape on the back of the corner piece, line up the upper left-hand corner with the lines, and press it down to keep it in place. Add matches as described in step 5. The confinement of the box walls will keep the top and left edges even.

Matches a go-go

13 Brush tacky craft glue on the bottom panel of the frame, in the space between the two corner pieces.

14 Starting next to the left corner, place five matches into the glue, burned ends facing in toward the frame opening. Flip the frame over to make sure that the matches overlap equally over the top and bottom edges. Adjust if necessary.

15 Place five more matches next to the last five, with the burned ends facing out.

16 To keep the pattern symmetrical, repeat steps 14 and 15 on the other end of the bottom panel. Continue working toward the center, alternating from end to end. When you reach the center, unless you have room for exactly five matches, add or subtract matches from the center group to keep the pattern symmetrical on either side of it.

17 Finish the other panels like this.

Finishing details

18 Brush tacky craft glue into the bare spot on the inner corner of each corner piece. Sprinkle in an embellishment of your choice, and pat it down. *(Gravel pictured.)*

19 Finish with two coats of amber varnish on the face of the frame. Wait between coats, per the directions on the varnish. *When you varnish, elevate the frame with a bottle-cap under each corner to keep it from sticking to whatever you have underneath it.*

When the varnish is dry

20 If you're using a transparent plastic panel in the frame opening, cut it ½" wider on all sides than the opening. On the backside of the frame, put a strip of double-sided tape along the top edge of the opening, and press the panel in place.

21 Mount the back panel to the frame. Seal it up with hot glue in the corners. Use self-adhesive loop-and-eye tape dots if you want to be able to change the picture.

variation

Flash fire fast frame: No extra corner pieces. No varnish. Start with a balsa wood plank, ¼" thick by 6" wide. Use a craft knife to cut a length that's right for your image. Cut out the opening. Assemble the back panel following Steps 7 to 10 above. Brush the face of the balsa with tacky craft glue. Begin with the bottom panel. Add three matches at a time, alternating between the left and the right side, making up any difference in the middle to keep the pattern symmetrical. For each group of three matches, alternate putting the burned ends facing in and facing out. Repeat on the top panel. On the side panels, turn the matches to run horizontally. Use tacky craft glue to add four matchsticks to the corners *(see photo below)*. Hot glue the back panel to the frame.

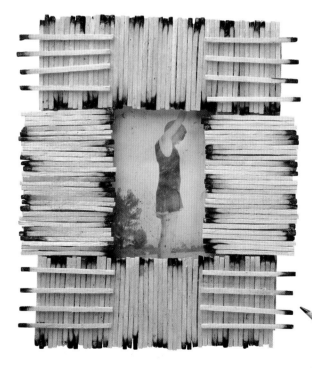

Quad City
Matchbox Drawers

Materials

4 matchboxes
Metallic gold acrylic paint
Hot glue
2 tiles *(preferably plastic)*
4 paper fasteners *(standard or mini)*
Adhesive felt
Sequins, rhinestones, and other decorations for top
Scrap of cardstock
Jeweler's epoxy
Toothpicks
2 cotton swabs
4 beads for legs

Tools

Paintbrush
Hot glue gun
Craft knife
Pencil
Scissors

There's a bit of beauty shop glamour to these. In the 1950s, they were used by suburban sophisticates as cigarette boxes, just a little extra something to put out for the guests. Vintage ones I've seen have always been made from plastic tile, but they work with ceramic tile, too. Patterned glass would be great, but be sure to have the glass-cutter smooth the edges.

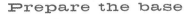

Prepare the base

1 Paint one face of each inner box in the matchbox gold. The inner box is the drawer.

2 Paint one outer side of each matchbox gold. If you plan to strike matches on it, paint around the strike plate.

3 Hot glue the matchboxes to the inside of one of the tiles, one box in each corner, gold sides facing out.

4 Hot glue the other tile on top of the matchboxes.

5 Make a small vertical slit in the center of each match drawer face. Insert a paper fastener and spread out the base to secure.

6 Line each drawer with a small piece of adhesive felt by tracing around the drawer onto the felt, trimming to size, and pressing in place. Slip the drawers back in the boxes, gold panel and drawer pull facing out.

7 Lay out a design with the decorations on the top tile, and put it in place with jeweler's epoxy. Mix the epoxy on a scrap of cardstock, and apply it with a toothpick. The designs pictured used sequins, flat-bottomed gems, bits of plastic flowers, and punched paper designs. *(Pick up small sequins and details with the dampened end of a cotton swab.)*

8 For the legs, epoxy the beads in place on the bottom.

A little trick when opening the drawers: Give the drawer behind the drawer you want to open a little push to help coax the drawer in front out.

Stitchin' for Everyone!

You don't have to be a tailor or seamstress, or even know how to hem a skirt to do the projects here. None of these require a sewing machine. The bath mitts on pages 132 and 133 could be finished with a machine, but they can be finished by hand as well.)

Did I mention that I don't sew? Thirty some years ago, I talked my school guidance counselor into letting me drop Home Economics and Gym so I could take more art classes. Consequently, I can't begin to thread a sewing machine, and I can't square dance. If I can make the projects in this section (and I did!), then even the most stitchin'-challenged among you can, too. (You'll have to find another book for the next hoedown, though.)

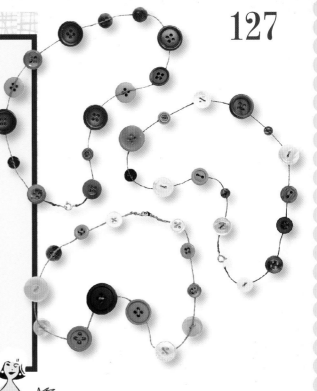

Quick as a wink

Button Necklace

Lay out about 15 buttons. Vary the size and color to suit your taste. Tie one end of a necklace closure to a 20" waxed linen thread. Pull the thread through a hole on the first button, from the back to the front, and then back through another hole, from the front to the back. Position the button about 1" from the closure, and tie a knot directly behind it. Continue with the rest of the buttons, tying them about 1" apart. Tie the other end of the closure about 1" from the last button. A spring ring clasp is shown, but any necklace clasp will do. Recycle one from a broken piece, or find one on a junking junket.

Leather Lacing 101

Your retro craft education would be lacking without the leather craft stitches at right, and the tips below for starting and finishing stitches. Turn the page for a couple of projects that will put that fancy-stitchin' skill to good use.

To start a stitch:

A few inches up from the end of the lacing, make two or three knots, enough to keep the end of the lace from going through the hole. Trim the tail to 2". Begin the stitch from the inside. Hold the tail and stitch over it to pin it in, or tuck it in afterward.

To finish a stitch:

Make one knot. Cut off the lacing 2" from the knot. Tuck the extra tail underneath the stitches.

Lacing required to Whip Stitch a seam:

About four times the seam length

NO.1 SINGLE-STRAND RUNNING STITCH

NO.2 TWO-STRAND RUNNING STITCH

NO.3 ONE-STRAND SPIRAL OR WHIP STITCH

NO.4 ONE-STRAND ALTERNATE SPIRAL

NO.5 VENETIAN SPIRAL OR WHIP

NO.6 ONE-STRAND BACK STITCH

NO.7 TWO-STRAND BRAIDED SPIRAL

NO.8 CROSS STITCH

NO.9 LOOP STITCH

Life's a stitch, so you better save some thread

At the risk of being a name-dropper, Sam the Sham said that to me, and I have to admit I don't have a clue what he meant—but I like the way it sounds. A few basic stitches will help you retro-embellish fabric, paper, or whatever else you can poke a needle through. Turn to page 132 for some embroidery stitches.

Seedy
Garden Box

Materials

10 empty seed packets
Cardstock
6" length of balsa wood plank, ¼" x 6"
Acrylic paint that matches the cardstock
Decorative paper *(optional)*
Glue stick
Punch template from page 129 copied on paper
Paper clips
Vinyl lacing
Hot glue
Alphabet letters to spell SEEDS

Tools

Ruler
Straightedge
Paintbrush
Craft knife
Small hole punch
Small tap hammer *(optional)*
Scissors
Hot glue gun

I love the graphics on seed packets. Maybe that's why I buy too many of them. What to do with all those packets of unplanted seeds, that make you feel guilty for never planting them? Make a box out of them to hide all the other seeds you haven't planted yet. Brilliant!

Cut

1 Measure the height and width of two seed packets laid side by side. That's the side panel measurement. Cut out four side panels from cardstock.

2 The length and width of the base are the same as the width of the side panels. Cut out the base.

3 The lid should be ½" longer and wider than the base panel. Cut out the lid.

To line or not to line

This box looked great made with black cardstock, no lining. But there was this retro-looking paper, printed to look like burlap, that was just begging to be paired with the seed packets. It added some extra steps and some extra time. You make the call whether or not you want to bother with a lining.

4 *If you're not lining the box:* Paint the sides and one face of the balsa panel to match the cardstock. Move on to step 7.

5 If you want to line the box:

Cut out four pieces of decorative paper the same size as the side panels, and one piece the same size as the base panel. Glue stick them in place.

For the lid, wrap one face and the sides of the balsa panel with decorative paper. Cut a strip to go on the box lid, under the alphabet lettering. Glue stick it in place.

Glue

6 Glue stick two seed packets to each side panel.

7 Glue stick seed packets to the lid, ¼" in from the side and bottom edges.

PUNCH TEMPLATE →

Punch List

SIDES: Both side edges and the bottom edge
1/8" holes at 1/4" intervals, inset 1/4" from the edge

BASE: All four side edges
1/8" holes at 1/4" intervals, inset 1/4" from the edge

LID: All four side edges
1/8" holes at 1/4" intervals, inset 1/2" from the edge

Get punchy

8 Punch! To do it yourself, make multiple copies of the *Punch Template* (those green dots at right). Use a paper clip to attach a template to each panel. Make the punches with a paper punch and tap hammer, or with a handheld punch.

Another option is to take the *Punch List, Punch Template,* lid, base, and side panels with you to an office services counter (found in most large office supply stores), or any-place that offers coil binding services. *(To make it easier, go over the Punch List with the person at the store who will be doing it. Consecutively punching pieces of the same length may save them from having to reset their equipment unnecessarily.)*

9 Whipstitch the side panels to the base. Lay the side panel facedown on the outer side of the base panel, lining up the bottom edges. Make the first stitch in the corner, following the *To start a stitch* on page 127. Be sure to stitch loosely enough so the panel can rotate upright when you're done.

10 Rotate the side panels up. Stitch the side seams.

11 Stitch the lid, with a single piece of lacing if possible.

Finish the lid

12 Hot glue the alphabet letters to the lid.

13 Hot glue the finished balsa panel to the inside center.

variation

Paint by Number Letter Box

Design something fun. Use at least three paint by number paintings. Pick ones that use similar or complementary colors and subject matter. For lively juxtaposition, mix things up so that adjoining pieces are from different paintings. Choose a center panel, like the horse, that can be cut around for an interesting edge.

To make a hanger, fold a colorful postcard in half along the short side, cut a 1½" strip from it, punch a hole about 3/8" from the top, hot glue the other end of it shut, and hot glue it dead center on the back of the box.

Beaded
Whimsey Pocket

Materials

Templates from page 171 copied on cardstock

Cereal box, or other light cardboard

Fabric

Spray adhesive

Scrap paper

Bead pattern copied from this page or a sketch of your own design

Tracing paper for fabric

Beads *(glass seed beads, sizes 8 to 11 work well)*

Extra strength thread

3" of ivory ribbon

Tools

Scissors

Pencil

Cardboard box for spraying, or drop cloth

Sewing needle

Beading needle, if using very small beads

Fine-point permanent marker

With seed beads, the higher the number, the smaller the bead. Size 10 and smaller beads require a special beading needle. Try to use larger beads, size 8 and 9, on the edges, since at some points there are several layers of cardboard to stitch through, and the heavier needle makes that easier.

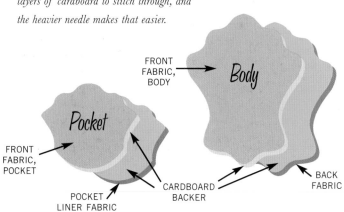

Plan your whimsey

1 The devil's in the details: Have swatches of fabric and your whimsey design with you when you shop for beads. It helps.

2 Look over the diagram at left to get an idea of how the whimsey is put together. The thread for beading is sewn through a facing fabric and a cardboard backing layer. For additional strength, there's another layer of cardboard behind that, which also provides a smooth surface for the backing fabric.

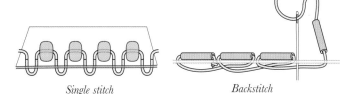

Single stitch   *Backstitch*

Cut, trace & cut

3 Cut out the templates. Trace two of each on the cardboard.

4 Cut out the cardboard backers.

5 Rough cut the fabric:

front fabric	7" x 9" piece	*(body)*
	7" x 6" piece	*(pocket)*
back fabric	7" x 9" piece	
pocket liner	7" x 6" piece	

Glue the backing in place

6 Mount each piece of fabric to a cardboard backer one at a time. Apply a light coat of spray adhesive to the cardboard (preferably the blank side, if there's printing on one side) and the back of the fabric. Press the cardboard and fabric with glued sides together, leaving a ³⁄₈" border of fabric all the way around. *(If you're using a heavy fabric, you can skip leaving a border and cut to exact size. You may want to brush the fabric edges with a product that prevents fraying. Go on to step 7, but skip step 8.)*

7 Flip the glued piece over onto a clean surface. Smooth from the center out toward the edges to remove any wrinkles or bubbles.

8 Use your thumb to push the excess fabric over onto the back of the cardboard. Follow the shape of the cardboard closely, allowing the fabric to overlap onto itself to accommodate the curves *(see photo below).*

Bead till you bleed

9 Sketch a bead pattern, using the one in the photo or one of your own design. Transfer it onto the front body and the front pocket pieces using the fabric tracing paper.

10 Most of the beading uses a single stitch. The edge beads are backstitched. To help plump up the wampum-shaped mound in the center of the bottom, there's a row of unseen beads underneath it, running in the other direction.

11 On the front pocket, bead everything but the side edges, stitching through the fabric and the cardboard backer it's mounted on. Start in the center and work out toward the edges.

12 As an extra something special, with a fine-point permanent marker, sign and date a piece of ivory ribbon. With the signature facing out and on the bottom, stitch the other end of the ribbon to the top center of the pocket liner. The ribbon will be hidden in the pocket, but can be pulled out, maybe years later, and read.

13 Apply spray adhesive to the back of the front pocket, and to the back of the pocket liner. Press together.

14 Bead everything on the front body but the edges.

15 Position the front pocket in place on the front body. Bead the edges of the pocket, attaching it to the body as you stitch. *This will be the toughest area to stitch, going through three layers of cardboard plus three layers of fabric.*

16 Continue beading the edges of the front body.

17 Make three sets of dangly loops for the bottom of the front body. Knot each set together, and leave 1" of extra thread at the end.

18 Apply spray adhesive to the cardboard backers on the front and back panels. Position the bead loops on the cardboard side of the back panel, and press the thread into the adhesive. Position the front body panel over it, and press it in place.

19 Stitch a 2" beaded loop to the top center of the back for a hanger.

20 It's a keeper. If you've never made a family heirloom before, you have now.

Woodland Friends
Wash Mitts

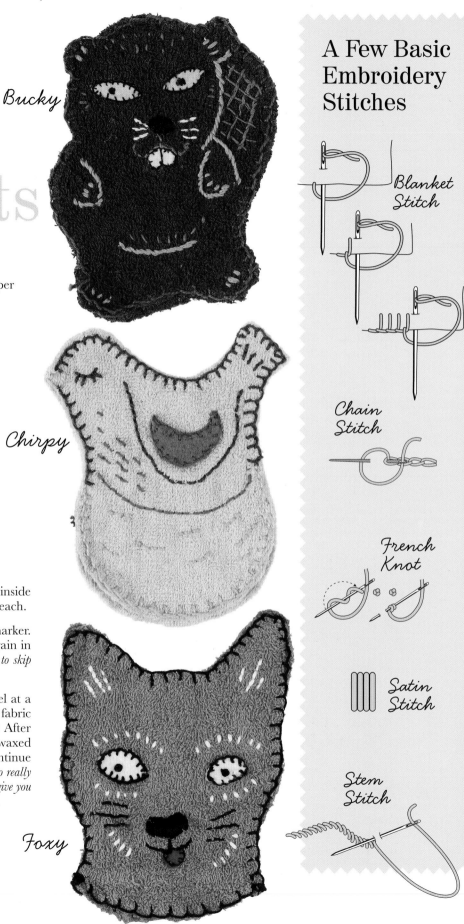

Bucky

Chirpy

Foxy

Materials

Templates from next page copied on tracing paper
Washcloths and/or towels in three colors
Straight pins
Waxed paper
Waterproof fabric glue or fray stopper
Felt
Embroidery floss

Tools

Scissors
Washable marker *(washable, as in washes out)*
Stiff-bristled brush for fabric glue
Embroidery needle
Tweezers

Get ready to stitch

1 Cut out the templates for the mitts.

2 Double up the washcloths or towels with the inside facing out. Pin a template through both layers on each.

3 Trace around the templates with washable marker. Remove the templates, and reserve them to use again in step 8. Cut the fabric along the lines. *If you prefer to skip the tracing and cut around the templates, by all means, do.*

4 Peel the front and back panels apart. One panel at a time, on the face of the fabric, brush a thin coat of fabric glue along all the cut edges. Work on waxed paper. After finishing each panel, put it on a fresh piece of waxed paper, glue side up. Toss out the gluey paper. Continue with all the panels. Set aside to dry. *Resist the urge to really pile the glue on; it doesn't take much. Using too much will give you an odd, rubbery edge and make it difficult to stitch through.*

A Few Basic Embroidery Stitches

Blanket Stitch

Chain Stitch

French Knot

Satin Stitch

Stem Stitch

Felt trims

5 Cut out the the felt trims for each mitt *(indicated with dotted lines on the templates at right)*:

> *Bucky*: Eyes and teeth

> *Chirpy*: Inset on wing

> *Foxy*: Eyes and tongue

6 Brush fabric glue on the back of the felt trims, and stick them in place on the front panel of each mitt.

Stitch the details

Be sure the edges are dry before continuing.

7 Blanket stitch around the felt trims.

8 Pin the template to the face of the front panel of each mitt and embroider the details on each, stitching through the tracing paper.

9 When you're done stitching, remove the pins from the template, and remove the paper. Use tweezers to remove any stubborn bits of paper that cling to the stitches, being careful not to pull any of the stitches or the loops in the terrycloth.

Stitch the panels together

Stitch the sides and top of the front panel to the back, leaving the bottom of the mitt open for wet, soapy hands.

10 Pin the front panels to the backs, placing the pins to avoid the outer edges, where the mitts will be stitched together.

11 Begin at the start point indicated on the template. Blanket-stitch around the right side, over the top, then down the left side, joining the front panel to the back as you stitch. Stop when you reach the *Stop-and-Drop* point on the left side *(indicated on the template)*.

Stitch the bottom edge

12 When you reach the *Stop-and-Drop*, drop the back panel and continue blanket stitching on the bottom edge of the front panel until you reach the starting point.

13 When you reach the starting point, tack a couple of stitches to reinforce that end of the opening. Then blanket-stitch back across the bottom of the back panel, until you reach the *Stop-and-Drop* point again. Tack a couple of stitches to reinforce that end of the opening. Knot off the thread, clip it, and you're done.

14 Get out the bubbles and run the bath.

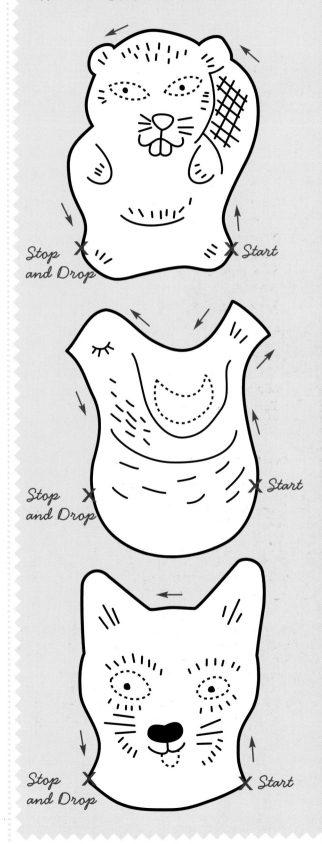

Templates
Copy on tracing paper at 230% to make 6" mitts.

Wacky Woodcraft

Wacky Woodcraft may be the only retro craft with a designated shelf in most thrift stores. There aren't any signs identifying it as such, but the plywood duck with the clothespin bill is a dead give-away. That may have something to do with the durability of wood projects. Wood holds up a whole lot better than construction paper and macaroni. And it may have something to do with the fact that for decades wood shop was a rite of passage for adolescent boys. In the mid-century years predating ATV vehicles and the NFL, plenty of dads and granddads spent their spare time in the home shop, churning out everything from simple, flat yard decorations to ornate and intricate shelves.

The projects in this section don't require a wood shop or a deep understanding of working with wood. For the most part, they require only simple, straight cuts. You could have those made when you buy the lumber—some places charge only a minimal cut fee.

For those of you interested in pursuing more wood projects, there are lots of vintage books and magazines with great ideas and detailed plans.

Quick as a wink! Snap Album

The dark brown felt on this album cover mimics the old wood-ornamented covers popular in the 1950s. Start with any photo album cover. This one was unfinished wood with ¾-inch binding posts that was purchased at a craft store. (First I sealed it with amber varnish.) Sketch your own design, or copy the one used here. Cut the paper pieces for the design out of paper. Cover the FRONT of each piece with spray adhesive, and place it face down on a sheet of dark brown felt. (The paper makes the felt easier to cut.) Cut out the paper-backed felt pieces with sharp scissors and arrange them on the album cover. Brush tacky craft glue on the paper backing and press the pieces in place on the cover. Fill the album with black paper. Mount the photos with old-fashioned paper corner mounts. Output digital pictures with at least ¼" of white border around the edges for a more retro look. If you want to get really Martha, trim the white borders with deckled specialty scissors.

Snappy Cappy

Bottlecap Man

Materials

3 wooden blocks *(as pictured: torso is $1^1/2$" D x $3^1/2$" W x 4" T, head is $1^1/2$" D x $1^1/2$" W by 2" T, base is $3/4$" thick x 5" square)*

Medium-grit sandpaper

Paint or stain

82 bottlecaps

Large nail

Masking tape

2 bowls

Trims for the face and head *(see note below)*

12-gauge wire

2 small wood screws

Tools

Paint brush

Small thick block of scrap wood
  (for pounding nails into)

Hammer

Drill

$1/4$" x 12" extra-long drill bit

Wire cutters

Needle-nose pliers

Screwdriver

The eyes are most often painted thumbtacks, but I've also seen buttons and brads. I used googly eyes because I was compelled to. Mouths are most often painted on or skipped altogether, but I've also seen buttons, red-coated wire, or red thumbtacks used.

The rings used for the ears and nose are often plastic curtain rings attached with tiny cup hooks, or screw eyes that were opened and then closed to hold the rings. Metal picture-hanger rings, frequently used on small decoupaged blocks, look smart, too. I attached curtain rings with a wire and cable stapler that shoots a round-crown staple that stands out slightly from the surface without cinching flat like a standard stapler.

Prep the wood

1 Sand the three wooden blocks just enough to smooth out the rough spots. Brush off the sawdust.

2 Paint or stain the blocks. Set aside to dry.

Prep the bottlecaps

3 Position a bottlecap, fluted side down, on the piece of scrap wood, and pound a nail through the center of the cap to make a hole. Pull the nail out, and repeat with all the other caps. Set aside.

Drill

To start a drill hole in an exact position on the wood, gently tap an indentation in that spot with the large nail. To drill to a specific depth, wrap masking tape around the bit at a point just above that measurement, making a little tab on the side of the bit with the ends of the tape. Drill until the tab touches the surface.

4 *Top bowl*: Drill a hole in the center of the bottom.

5 *Bottom bowl*: Drill three holes in the bottom bowl: one where you plan to attach the bowl to the torso, and another on each side of that where you will attach the arms. *To avoid any danger of the edge of the rim snapping away, drill the holes about 1/2" down from the top edge.*

6 *Base*: Drill holes for the legs in the bottom of the base, about 1/4" deep, 1" in from the sides, and centered from front to back.

7 *Head*: Flip the head upside down, and drill a hole about 1/2" deep into the center of the bottom side of the head block.

8 *Torso*: For the neck, drill a hole about 2" deep into the top of the torso block. It should be set back slightly from the center so that the neck wire doesn't hit the arm wire below it. For the legs, drill two holes in the bottom of the torso block, each about 1" in from the sides and about 1" deep. For the arms, drill a hole, starting about 3/4" down from the top edge on one side of the torso block, clear through to the other side.

Making faces

9 Choose one of the methods listed below the tool list, or create your own to give the man a face.

Get wired

10 Cut a 2" length of wire for the neck, a 20" length of wire for the arms, and two 5" lengths of wire for the legs.

11 Gently tap the leg wires into the base.

12 Add 20 bottlecaps to each leg wire.

13 Insert the end of each leg wire into the holes drilled in the bottom of the torso. To help secure the legs, press down hard on his shoulders, then pick him up, still holding his shoulders, and smack him down a couple of times on his base.

14 Use the needle-nose pliers to bend one end of the arm to form a small, open loop (large enough to slip the lower bowl onto).

15 Stack 20 bottlecaps on the arm, pushing them up against the looped end. Thread the unlooped end of the arm wire through the hole in the side of the torso. Add 20 bottlecaps to the other side. Bend that end of the arm wire into a small, open loop, and trim off the excess.

16 Gently bend an elbow-like curve into the arm wire.

Heads up

17 Tap the neck wire into the head.

18 Attach the top bowl to the head with a screw.

19 Slip a bottlecap onto the neck wire, and put the wire into the hole in the top of the torso.

Finish it up

20 Slip the lower bowl onto the ends of the arm wires. Futz with the bowl and the arms till the bowl is level and held close against the front of the torso.

21 Screw the lower bowl in place.

22 Use the needle-nose pliers to gently close the ends of the arms wires.

23 Add buttons or ornaments to the front of the torso.

24 Put your Calypso inspired cap-man to use.

Collector/curator William Swislow (pages 16 and 17) amassed a formidable army of bottlecap men. Check out the wealth of information and imagery he's put together at http://www.interestingideas.com/out/cap.htm

Old School
Spool Shelves

Materials

3 wooden planks, 24" x 6" x ³/₈"
Ebony wood stain
Stack of old newspaper
86 wooden spools
Waxed paper
4 pieces of ¹/₄" x ¹/₄" basswood, or
  small round dowels, 1" long
Bailing wire *(16 gauge, dark annealed)*
Extra-long nail or a plant hanger

Tools

Drill and ¹/₈" wood drill bit
Rubber gloves
Brush for stain
Rags
Wire cutters
Snub-nose pliers

If you want your shelves to look old, use old spools and old wood for the planks. For new wood, distress it with a chain or wire brush, and use a specialty paint for a crackled effect. Consider finishing the completed shelves with a coat or two of amber varnish.

Anchor pinned in place

The older shelves I've collected are all made with these shapely spools. I ordered mine online searching for "wood spools, craft supplies" (without the quotes). I used ⁷⁄₈" x 1¹⁄₈" because they were substantially cheaper than the next size up.

Prep

1 Drill a hole in each of the corners of each of the shelf planks. For the ⁷⁄₈" diameter spools pictured, the holes were set in about ⁷⁄₈" from the sides of the boards.

2 Apply wood stain to the shelf planks following the directions on the product you're using. Wear rubber gloves and cover your work area with newspaper.

3 Stain the spools. Set aside on waxed paper. *Faced with the daunting task of staining a big pile of spools, I came up with a method that, although not very precise, worked well enough for me. I put on the rubber gloves, poured a puddle of stain in a rag, and one at a time, put a spool in the rag and squeezed my fist shut. I blotted the excess off each spool with a different rag, and set the spool aside to dry. The spools I used grabbed the stain and only needed one quick coat.*

4 Stain the four 1" lengths of basswood. These will be the anchor pieces that hold the wire beneath the bottom shelf.

Allow all the stained wood to dry according to the directions on the product.

Fuss with the wire

5 Cut four lengths of wire, 50" long.

6 Bend the last 3" of each piece of wire up against itself, forming a small loop on the bent end.

7 On each corner of the bottom shelf plank, push the bent end of a wire piece through the hole. Slip one of the 1" anchor pieces into each loop, then pull the wires tightly up against the bottom of the shelf, pinning the anchors in place *(see arrow above)*.

8 Thread eight spools onto each of the wires. (The open ends of the bent wire will tuck inside the first few spools.)

9 Add the second shelf plank.

10 Add six spools, then the top shelf plank.

11 Hold together the ends of the two wires on the left side of the shelves. Thread 15 spools over both wires. Position the bottommost spool close to the shelf plank, centered from front to back.

12 Repeat for the right side of the shelves.

Twistin'

13 After centering the top wires over the shelves, grip all four wires with snub-nose pliers and twist them together, beginning at the point where the top spools meet in the center and continuing to the ends of the wire.

14 Bend the twisted wire to make a loop, about 3" tall, and wrap the remaining wire tightly around the base of it. If there is any excess, clip it off with the wire cutters and press the ends down against the loop.

Hangin' out

15 These shelves need to be hung a couple of inches out from the wall in order to hang straight and not angle out. Use an extra-long nail or a plant hanger.

Long on Style
Yardstick Organizers

Materials

2 yardsticks
18" x 3" wood panel, 3/16" thick
Tiny brads, 1/2" long

Tools

Pencil
Straightedge
Saw
Hammer

The project shown was made from two yardsticks.
The vintage piece pictured below was made with one yardstick
and no additional wood. The base is a piece of the yardstick
so the side panels are shorter.

1 Cut two 18" lengths of yardstick.

2 Attach the base to the side panels. Tap brads through the backside of the base, every 3" or so.

3 Measure the space between the two side panels. From the remaining yardstick, cut to fit two end panels and as many divider pieces as you'd like.

4 Tack the end and divider panels in place with brads. Tap them through from the underside of the base, using four brads for each panel.

5 Fill it with fun stuff, or set one out empty and see how fast it fills up. Make one with a single divider in the center to hold remotes near the television. Placed near the computer, they make a warm counterbalance to all the wires and putty-colored plastic. From time to time, mine actually gets pressed into service to measure things.

Oh Canada, My Hands Are Wet
Towel Holder

Materials

Leaf-shaped piece of wood*
Acrylic paint** *(optional)*
Small brads, 7/8" long
2, short, 1/2-inch-diameter sticks *(dowels or wood scraps)*
Wood glue
4" length of 1/4" x 1/2" basswood stick *(or other wood scrap)*
Amber varnish
Hanger *(27" tasseled curtain tie-back pictured)*

Tools

Wood-burning tool**
Paintbrush** *(optional)*
Pencil
Hammer
Rag
Foam brush
Staple gun

*** This piece is embellished with wood burning, but the details on the leaf could be painted in, if you prefer.*

Jazz it up a little

1 Wood burn or paint details on the front of the leaf.

2 Mark the placement of the towel bar supports, 2" or so above the bottom edge of the leaf and 4" to 6" apart.

3 Tap the brads for the towel bar supports through from the back of the leaf till they begin to come out the front.

4 Stand up a towel bar support, apply glue to the top of it, and position it under the leaf so that the brad will come through the center of it. Finish tapping the brad through the back of the leaf and into the support until the support is attached firmly in place. Wipe up any glue if it oozes out. Repeat with the other support.

5 Flip the leaf onto its back. Apply glue to the exposed ends of the towel bar supports. Center the towel bar over the supports, and attach it to the supports using brads. Wipe up any excess glue.

6 Apply two coats of amber varnish, following the directions on the can.

After it dries

7 Add the hanger to the back. *(For the tasseled tie-back hanger pictured, I doubled it up, pulling one tassel lower than the other. Then I tied a knot to form a hanging loop at the top, and stapled it to the back of the leaf several times through the knot.)*

Leaf-shaped wood pieces aren't too hard to find in craft stores. Cutting it out by hand with a coping saw is an option. (Baking a pan of brownies for your favorite wood worker is another.) Use a 8" x 8" wood panel, anywhere from 1/8" to 1/2" thick. Copy this page at 160% and use the project photo as a template.

Chapter 5

Continuing Education

To buy or not to buy

Strength in numbers

An army of cheery pine cone elves, a window full of sparkling decoupage glass, a spare sofa overrun with a tangle of gangly sock monkeys—collecting multiple examples of the same retro craft is just plain fun. In addition to the visual merriment, having multiples can help illuminate, inform, and inspire you when you're making your own version.

When in Rome

Take advantage of regional influences when you're hunting retro crafts. Shellcraft is the catch of the day near the seashore, while twig furniture is prevalent in rural areas (maybe that's why they call it "The Sticks"). Driftwood sculptures are common in communities along the Great Lakes.

Make 'em laugh

Some retro craft defies logic, and that in itself is an endearing quality. If you can't look at a particular piece without smiling, why not bring it home and put it somewhere where it can cheer you up when you need it? Try it next to the washing machine, near your bill paying area, or maybe by the bathroom scale.

The Lumpy Twins
Hand-built ceramics
10 inches tall
These ceramics class cast-offs came from the same thrift store shelf, but were made and signed by two different people. Either one makes me smile, and collectively they crack me up.

Aunt Betty readies the punch bowl
Oh, I'm pulling your leg. I'd like to claim this exuberantly decorated room was put together by kin, but it's really the "Burl Room" at the Henry Cowell Redwoods State Park in Santa Cruz, California.

Why Collect?

Why Not & Why Fer

Many of you, like me, collect retro craft for one simple reason: you can't stop yourself. But you don't have to be a folded-paper-handbag-toting craft fanatic to enjoy the benefits of collecting. There are more practical, less obsessive reasons.

Collecting retro craft objects and publications is a great way to find additional projects to make. Original printed directions are your "Easy Pass" to retro crafting. Having an original, or instructions for how to make it, can save you the time and trouble of reinventing the wheel when you want to replicate your grandmother's Perky Pinecone Elves for all of the cousins. Having an actual piece will not only bring to life what's on the page, but close scrutiny may reveal some secrets to how it's best

made. Like peanut butter and chocolate, original directions and original pieces complement one another, but either, in the absence of the other, is still a valuable resource in making retro craft.

Decorating with retro craft is easy and fun. Collected pieces displayed in your living or work space (in moderation or excess) can lend a sense of warmth, a touch of levity, or even an air of mystery to the environs. (More living with retro craft ideas are in chapter 6.)

Collecting for profit can also be a rationale, but only for the extremely patient investor with modest expectations. The formal art world can barely bring itself to peek at the googly-eyed realm of retro craft. Despite encouraging steps forward like the *Outside the Lines*

show at Intuit Gallery, a retro craft wing at the Museum of Modern Art is a long way off. Not to say retro crafts haven't appreciated in value—they have. Bottlecap men that used to guard the shelves at thrift stores are now sporting tony price tags in upscale retro stores and antique malls. But if your motive is monetary gain, investing in a financial instrument of a more typical sort is surely a better bet, and won't require dusting. The most important "why" in your collection should always be the affection you feel for the things you acquire.

What to Collect

Retro Craft Pieces

As with all collecting, you should acquire pieces that appeal to your personal aesthetic. How do you know what that is? An inner voice will tell you. That voice is your Inner Aesthetician.

Hearing voices isn't necessarily a bad thing. You may walk past a retro craft object that intrigues you even though you have no idea why. The thing that makes you do a double take is your Inner Aesthetician. It's saying, "Hey, this is swell, isn't it?" You may take a closer look and decide it's not for you, and walk on. But if you pass by again and once more that piece catches your eye, it's because your Inner Aesthetician is now jumping up and down and screaming at you. Go home without it and you're almost sure to get a bad case of the should-have-bought-it regrets.

Collect things that you want to live with. Collect things that strike sentimental chords, that conjure happy memories. Collect things that you want to learn from. Collect things that incorporate materials or ideas that you would like to include in your own work. Collect things that make you smile or even laugh out loud.

Collect what inspires you.

Fez and Mystic Shrine symbol wall ornaments
Wood marquetry
6 x 5 inches, 4 x 5 inches

Retro Craft Magazines, Pamphlets & Books

I remember the day in my childhood when I realized that people don't live in the places where they work. I had thought that, at the end of the day, the people at the bank walked through the stylish white flagstone lobby, ambled up the curved, suspended staircase, and were home; the doctor slept on a cold, paper-covered aluminum table in the back of his office; and the gas station attendant grabbed a key with a giant plank of wood dangling from it, and retired to a room in the back of his "house" with the big green plaster dinosaur out front. It was a true lightbulb moment when I learned this was not so.

Years later, flipping through a vintage magazine, I came across directions for making a hideously flawed, make-you-scratch-yourself-on-the-head-and-say-"What?" scrap craft object. Once again I experienced a lightbulb moment. For years I had collected vintage craft objects, the more odd and flawed the better. I happened to have one of the same hideously flawed, make-you-scratch-yourself-on-the-head-and-say-

"What?" scrap craft objects pictured in the magazine. I was stunned to see directions detailing the construction of what appeared to be such a haphazard thing. I had assumed mine had emerged by happenstance from various art-making remnants that had accumulated on somebody's work desk. I was amazed to learn that it was born instead of fastidiously followed written directions. It was in that lightbulb moment that my obsession with collecting retro craft objects extended to collecting vintage publications with printed directions for making them.

Macaroni Poodle courtesy Amos Craft Publishing, Sidney, OH 45365 USA
From *Pack-o-Fun* magazine, January 1967

This enchanting novelty poodle, with his life-like macaroni coat, is a real conversation piece—your friends will love him!

Among the many varieties of macaroni, we found types perfectly shaped for our poodle's curly coat. All you need do is glue them to a simple cardboard body.

Cut lightweight cardboard into pieces of the shape and size shown in the drawings, for the different parts of the poodle.

Roll the body into a cone-like cylinder and tape or glue to hold. Roll

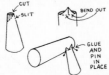

the front legs in the same way; tape at a slight angle to the wide end of

the body. Roll up the back legs; then cut off at top as shown by dotted line.

PACK-O-FUN

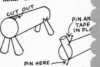

Make a ¼" vertical slit at highest point. To form tabs, bend out cardboard at sides of slit. Glue and tape the legs to body, as shown. To make the dog stand squarely, trim legs if needed.

Roll the neck, lengthwise, and ... to hold. Cut out a small curved ...

... tion at the top front of the body ... sert the neck, as shown; then p... glue in place.

Roll up the tail, lengthwi... insert at an angle into a sma...

... cut in the top back of the bo... and pin in place. Add a tin... foam ball at the tip.

For the head, use a 3" plas... ball. Cut an opening to p... onto the neck, gluing in pl... the poodle's nose, cut a sm...

BODY   FRONT
NECK   TAIL   NOSE

JANUARY 1967   17

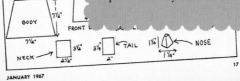

Making Choices

When you begin collecting retro craft books, you'll discover there are some books that require no deliberation whatsoever. You see one on a table at a yard sale, and from the cover you can just tell it's going to be chock-full of projects you can't wait to try. Try your best not to lunge. Barring that, make your lunge for the book as graceful as possible.

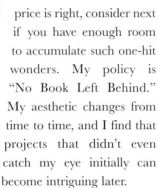

Sometimes there may be just one or two projects that appeal to you out of an entire book full of them. If the price is right, consider next if you have enough room to accumulate such one-hit wonders. My policy is "No Book Left Behind." My aesthetic changes from time to time, and I find that projects that didn't even catch my eye initially can become intriguing later.

When looking at retro craft publications, think about ways to alter projects to make them work best for you. Keeping the concept of the project in mind, visualize changing the materials to evoke an era you prefer, or changing the scale to make a project larger or smaller.

Looking for *Craft Instructions* Outside the Box in All the Wrong Places

Look beyond craft specific publications when you're hunting for magazines and books with retro craft projects. Craft instructions were tucked into all kinds of pop-culture publications. Bible and Sunday school manuals often include simple craft projects for kids. Many vintage cookbooks had tips for fabulous table decor to be created by the consummate crafty hostess. (The era of easy-to-make recipes left some time to kill between plopping the canned soup in the pan and tossing in the wiener slices.) Even oddball publications like General Motors' periodical *Motoring* featured craft projects.

Slight adjustments can make a big difference. Vintage holiday publications are brimming with projects that you can take the ho-ho-holiday out of by changing the materials and colors used. Many include plenty of gift making ideas with no holiday theme.

Some books that lack inspiring projects may have very informative general hints or how-to sections. Check the index and leaf through the back. Because books dedicated to crafts have more room to fully expand on a topic than periodicals or pamphlets, they frequently include well-illustrated, step-by-step instructions detailing obscure or near-forgotten techniques that may be of use to you.

Tin Can Projects for Children and all images opposite page, courtesy of Amos Craft Publishing, Sidney, OH 45365 USA, From *Pack-o-Fun* magazine, May 1964, January 1965, January 1967, February 1967, May 1967, May 1968

Pack·o·Fun

These people were having way too much fun! Fueled by the creativity of Edna Clapper and published by her husband, John, *Pack-o-Fun* debuted in 1951. The elder Clappers stepped down in 1974, but the magazine is still running.

Vintage issues featured dozens of projects, all wonderfully creative, some ingeniously practical and others pathologically impractical. Once subtitled *The Only Scrap-Craft Magazine*, issues from that era had projects made from anything most folks would throw in the trash (egg cartons, plastic bottles, old greeting cards, plastic berry baskets) and then some. Changes in packaging have made some of these once-bountiful materials all but extinct, but using a little creativity, these clever ideas can be adapted with modern castoffs.

Issues of *Pack-o-Fun* from the 1950s and '60s featured ads for scores of craft books and pamphlets, and are great places to research retro craft publication titles. Be sure to check out regular features including *Idea Exchange*, *Edna's Mail*, and *Pen Pals*. (In one of my favorite *Pen Pal* entries, in 1968 a 12-year-old girl from Montana listed "psychedelic decorating" as one of her hobbies.)

One word of caution when buying online, there is another vintage magazine with a very similar name, *Pack O' Fun*. Note the capital "O" with an apostrophe behind it. It features risqué girly cartoons.

Where to Look

Home Is Where the Heart-Shaped Candy Box Made into a Picture Frame Is

If your mother is the sentimental type, your early work may still be gracing her shelves. (If not, it may be gracing someone else's shelves, a quirky yard sale purchase years ago.) Let family members know you're interested in vintage crafts. Many families had an adult crafter or two. For some it might have been a brief infatuation with all things sparkly, for others a long-term love affair as evidenced by bins full of plastic foam balls, sequins, beads, and geegaws. Your family crafters may be "out"—the jigsaw puzzle piece reindeer pin with googly eyes or the crocheted poodle toilet paper cover are dead giveaways. Or they may be closet crafters who have long since shelved their pipe cleaners.

Odds are your crafty family member may still have some of his projects, supplies, and publications. Vintage crafts promote a pack-rat mentality. Retired or still gluing, your Great Aunt Crafty will probably be more than happy to talk retro craft with you. If retired, she may be thrilled to pass on her crafting vestiges to someone who will appreciate them and put them to use. Nothing makes a pack rat happier than when something she's saved for 30 years turns out to serve a useful purpose. (Can you embroider, "I told you so?" If not, just spell it out in macaroni.)

The Usual Suspects

Wherever you find household castoffs, you'll find retro craft: yard sales, antique malls and shops, estate sales, auction houses, eBay, and the trash trifecta—junk shops, thrift stores, and flea markets. As a general rule, things are less expensive at the bottom of the junk pyramid, with yard sales having the biggest bargains. Prices tend to go up in this order: yard sales, junk shops/thrift stores/flea markets, estate sales, auctions, and antique malls and stores. It's a topsy-turvy world, and there are always exceptions to the rule. Auction prices (both online and live) can fluctuate from the top to the bottom of the scale, screaming deals can be found at antique malls, and sometimes the ridiculously high prices at a yard sale lets you know the seller has seen one too many episodes of *Antiques Roadshow*.

The pyramid reverses when considering your odds for finding retro craft. Antique shops and malls may charge more, but usually are well peppered with a broad variety of pieces and publications, even supplies. Be prepared for items there to be labeled "folk art" with price tags to match. Although retro crafts may be harder to find at yard sales, they're more likely to be thought of as white elephants and priced accordingly. Be ready for the folks selling them to do a little jig or end-zone dance when you pay them greenback dollars for something they consider oddball and worthless.

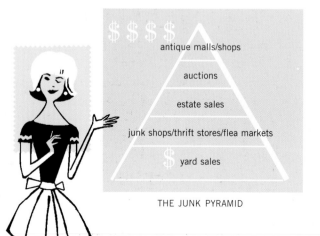

$$\$\$\$\$$$

antique malls/shops

auctions

estate sales

junk shops/thrift stores/flea markets

$ yard sales

THE JUNK PYRAMID

Above right: **Crocheted Poodle Toilet Paper Cover,** Yarn, googly eyes, ribbon, 12 inches tall
Opposite: Pin cushion courtey of Amos Craft Publishing, Sidney, OH 45365 USA, From *Pack-o-Fun* magazine, January 1965

The How

Learning from Retro Craft Publications

If you've ever used a recipe from a vintage cookbook, you may know that sinking feeling of being up to your elbows in flour and baking soda, when suddenly the recipe requires something entirely out of left field, not even mentioned in the list of ingredients. Crafting from vintage directions can be a lot like that. It's always worthwhile to read the directions all the way through before purchasing supplies or starting a project. Make sure that any supply or tool mentioned in the text is also in the supply list (and on your shopping list). The directions may offer information that will influence your supply and tool choices, or recommend substitutes not mentioned in the supply list.

As your retro craft publication library grows, you'll have the luxury of reviewing different directions for making similar projects. Note the constants and the variables. Glean what you want from each technique, and create your own approach.

Occasionally vintage craft directions will call for a material that is not-so-readily available anymore, or for which it would make a lot more sense to use something new that didn't exist back when the directions were written. Don't be afraid to improvise. Like a civil war reenactor comfortable in his inauthentic but unseen contemporary underwear, I don't sweat over absolute authenticity. I make retro craft using modern tools and supplies that mimic the original materials.

Learning from Retro Craft Pieces

If you have examples of the craft you're about to embark on—actual pieces or photographs—take a good look at them. Study them without assumptions about how they were made. If you look at the object with fresh eyes, you may discover something that can help you when you're making it.

Having more than one example of the same project is all the merrier, especially if they were made by different crafters. Multiple pieces can show you multiple choices for materials or different ways of assembling those materials.

The Retro Craft Autopsy

You may be able to learn what you need to know just by giving a piece a careful look, or with minimal intrusion. Sometimes I find it necessary to sacrifice a vintage piece to learn more about how it was made. Curious if there was a way to make my own compressed cotton heads, I once took a craft knife to the noggin of a pinecone elf, may his fake-snow-crusted soul rest in piece. (I love those little bobbly-headed guys desperately, and taking a knife to one wasn't easy. It didn't help that my significant other made excruciating squealing noises as I cut.) I learned there was no base material inside, just densely spun cotton around a hollow center.

Some pointers if you decide to dissect:

- *You may be able to find out what you'd like to know without destroying the whole piece. Take apart a small section first. Follow my mother's rule for ironing; start in a less conspicuous place, if possible, maybe the back or bottom side.*

- *Keep a tray handy to put all the little bits and pieces in as you disassemble so they don't get lost or misplaced.*

- *If you keep an Idea Box (page 33), make notes about what you learn, and file them in the box.*

- *If the piece can't be put back together, reuse its components.*

Assembly Required

Crafting in Numbers

Getting together with like-minded crafters is a great way to further your retro craft education. Besides being a whole lot of fun, a craft group is a swell place to share ideas and resources such as books, magazines, supply sources, and more. Seeing all the different approaches to the same project can be inspirational.

Meeting with a group helps keep the momentum going. When you're working alone, it's easy to find other things that seem to need your attention more urgently than the unfinished craft project collecting dust in the corner. Being part of a group that meets regularly helps you to set aside time just for crafting. Also, most of us are more likely to keep a commitment that involves other people than one made just to ourselves.

If you're interested in finding a craft group in your area, start by asking friends and colleagues. Check the bulletin board at your local art and craft stores, coffeehouse, or bookstore, etc. Search the meetings section of your local paper. Check the internet. There are special websites to help people find local groups or individuals with similar interests. Finding a retro craft specific group will probably be difficult. You can still enjoy the fun and camaraderie of crafting in numbers by joining a non-retro group. Take pride in your petunia-in-the-onion-patch status as the rogue retro crafter.

Or start your own retro group! Spread the word among friends, post a notice in vintage clothing or furniture stores, or advertise in any of the places just mentioned.

Deciding What Works Best for Your Group

There's no magic formula for organizing a group that works for everyone. A working group will be tailored to fit the needs of the individuals in it, taking into account their proximity, interests, timetables, and lifestyles. There will be hitches and glitches, but discussing some of the variables and making choices about them in the beginning can make things smoother. And be open to tweaking and adjusting as the members and their needs change over time.

Here are some useful things to consider when organizing a group.

1. How often will you meet, and how long will each meeting last?

2. What day will you meet on?

3. Where will you meet?

4. How will you contact one another between meetings?

5. Are RSVPs required?

6. What projects will you do?

7. Will the group have a leader, rotate leaders with projects, or operate by consensus?

8. Will you limit the size of the group?

9. Are children or any other guests welcome?

10. Will you have food and drink?

11. Will you share expenses for any tools or supplies?

12. Will you charge dues or fees?

Other Considerations

Once the group is off the ground, here are things you can do to enhance your craft group experience.

Bring in personal projects. *This is a great way to get feedback from fellow crafters, and if you finish the group project early (or abandon it altogether), you'll have something else to do.*

> "...discussing some of the variables & making choices about them in the beginning can make things smoother."

Keep things festive. *We approach our gatherings as if they were cocktail parties with projects. A little extra effort in planning goes a long way toward making things fun.*

Use reference pieces. *Find examples or pictures of the crafts you're going to be making. Set them out before you begin your projects. Look them over and talk about what they're made of and the different ways they were put together. Your group may come across a new approach to make things simpler or better. And if unexpected problems come up while you're working, it's nice to have actual physical pieces to refer to.*

Discuss group business mid-meeting. *Because people sometimes show up late and leave at different times, it's best to discuss group business mid-meeting or whenever the most members are present.*

Take a retro craft field trip! *How about a craft day overnight at a not-too-far-away retro motel? You can swim, relax, go junking, have a twist party in your room, and eventually work on projects. Pick a project that requires a minimum of tools and supplies, so you don't have to drag half the studio with you. (See "Retro Craft-a-Go-Go" page 167.)*

Retro craft outreach. *Your group may want to volunteer to conduct a craft class at a local nursing home, hospital, or other facility. You may find yourself learning more from your students than you teach, especially at the nursing home.*

Ladies of the Blue Ridge Craft Clatch (that's not a typo) enjoying the potluck buffet

Workstations

Setting up designated workstations for certain things helps keep order in what can very quickly become chaos. Scattering them throughout the work area will help disperse activity and keep any one spot from becoming too congested. Stock them with the appropriate tools and supplies.

You may come up with other workstations that make sense for your group; the ones we use most are:

Cutting Station — *Sturdy table, self-healing cutting mat, straightedge, craft knife and blades, scissors, and a trash can for scraps. If there are supplies shared by everyone (paper, board, etc.), locate these supplies near the cutting station.*

Glue Station — *Something to protect the work surface from spills, plenty of scrap paper, glues, electrical access for glue guns, and paper towels and/or handy wipes for clean up*

Glitter Station — *Stack of scrap paper, glitters, and glitter station directions (page 51)*

Quick as a wink

Reminder Booklet

Make sweet little felt booklets for the members of your group to hold notepaper and a reminder card with upcoming Craft Day dates. Cut a piece of felt, 2¾" x 8½". Glue the reminder card inside. Hole punch a stack of 12 pieces of scratch paper, 2½" x 3¾" and hold them in place with a brad. Pink the bottom edge and customize each with a pinked initial.

It's Craft Day! It's Craft Day!

People get ready

Whether it's a group leader, a meeting host, or each member collectively pitching in, your get-togethers will require a little prep.

Set up the worktable(s). I like to cover the whole table with a disposable plastic tablecloth, and then put a scrap paper "place mat" in front of each crafter. The place mats keep the tablecloths clean enough to reuse a few times, and they help define everyone's work space. Use what's cheap and handy to make the place mats: pages from gossip magazines are fun, paper towels or waxed paper are easy.

Set out stacks of small paper plates on the worktables that crafters can use for glue, paint, and work materials they don't want to lose in the clutter.

Print out or copy any project directions or templates.

Read the project directions and put out jars of water and rags if painting, extra trash bags if cutting paper, scrap paper if gluing. If you have the space, set up workstations (see left) for specific activities.

Have on hand an extra power strip and extension cord or two. They can save the craft day, especially when the glue guns come out.

If your craft day includes food, set out whatever you need (dishes, napkins, etc.), so that chasing those things down doesn't cut into your craft time.

Packing your stuff

Read through the project directions and imagine the process, anticipating what tools or materials not mentioned might make things easier.

Let the crafting commence

While you're working, take a time-out now and then to look at your fellow crafters' projects as they progress.

Be delighted, not discouraged, by master crafters in your group.

Have a show-and-tell at the end of Craft Day. Taking pictures of everyone's project and keeping a scrapbook for the group is both fun and useful.

Learn From Our Mistakes

This is definitely do-as-I-say-and-not-as-I-do territory. When my group started, none of us had ever been part of a craft group before. What follows is a laundry list of our early missteps so you can try to avoid them:

Mistake #1 *Trying to undertake too many projects in a single meeting.* Our first craft day was a Christmas Craftacular. I picked out and bought supplies for—count 'em—13 projects! It was nuts. Most people finished just one or two projects. It was crazy fun, but it was crazy hard work, too, and expensive.

Mistake #2 *Not giving enough advance notice of the meeting.* We tried pulling things together last minute and called meetings with only a week's notice, but that made it harder for members to make necessary family or work arrangements to accommodate a day off.

Mistake #3 *Not announcing the project ahead of time.* Not giving advance notice of the project made the organizer responsible for getting all supplies (disorganizer, in some cases, and yes, that was me plenty of times). Announcing the project ahead of time provides time to think about the project and come up with ideas, discuss it, and get together all the needed tools and supplies.

Mistake #4 *Not making copies of the project directions.* No matter how small the group, having a copy of the project directions for each crafter makes working a lot easier.

Mistake #5 *Not having enough tools.* There were never enough scissors, never, ever! Everything flows more smoothly when people come equipped with their own tools.

On Keeping Things Retro

- **Choose projects** *that come from retro publications, are inspired by retro craft objects, or include retro imagery.*

- **Vintage records** *and a portable record player keep the party going. Ours is spinning from the moment we step inside the door till the last scrap-o-paper is swept from the floor.*

- **Vintage aprons** *add an extra touch. Besides being functional, the colors, fabrics, and hand-ornamentation are all retro-inspirational.*

Chapter 6

Retro Craft Living

Retro Craft Reuse

Hand-crafted bowls and baskets can collect mail, unfiled CDs, or whatever household detritus has a habit of accumulating.

A key holder doesn't need to hold keys. Use one next to the stove to hold a few favorite kitchen utensils.

Need a tray? They're useful on the bar, in the kitchen, and on the vanity. Put handles on a spare frame to make one in a flash (page 112).

Napkin holders are great letter organizers. If you can't find one at the flea market, you must be walking through with your eyes closed.

Use a wall pocket as an "emergency" penholder. It's like the fire extinguisher in the glass case, ready and waiting when you're truly in a fix.

Ditch the picture of the white-tailed deer that was in it. Fire up the glue gun and your imagination to give a pine slice frame a new life.

Opposite, top: Retro craft and folk art commingle with musical memorabilia in my living room.

Opposite, below: **Mismatched doggie bookends**
Wood, stain
7 x 7 inches

Putting Your Tsatske to Task

Making the Frivolous Functional

I like to find practical uses for what I collect, partly because space is at a premium in my domicile, making functionality a plus, and partly to assuage my guilt over my compulsive collecting (as if my husband really believes I need that ceramics-class-project-gone-wrong to hold paperclips). It may seem like artistic sacrilege to some, like hanging coats on the Venus de Milo, but to tell the truth, if the Venus de Milo was in my house, I probably would hang coats on her. I like the ingenuity and incongruity of using things outside the realm of their original purpose.

A hand-hewn birdhouse caboose put to reuse in the kitchen, both as a bookend, and as a caddy for coffee equipment

true rarity. It's much more common to find frayed cords, dangerous, squirrelly plugs, and faulty switches and sockets. Don't take chances—always have lamps evaluated and repaired by a trained professional before putting them to use.

Retro craft shelves can be a stylish and inexpensive alternative to bland fiberboard or metal shelving. There are a lot of them out there. They were a favorite home-shop project, and for generations the dads and grand-dads of America cranked out bumper crops. The no-assembly-required factor is pretty appealing. Would you rather browse through junk shops looking for fun and fanciful shelves, or spend half your afternoon in the super-sized home store and the other half on your floor with a pile of screws and a complex exploded view assembly chart? The poorly translated directions can be amusing, but I'd pick junking any day.

Making your own shelves is an option too. Check out the Wooden Spool Shelves, page 138. They can hold a lot and go together in a flash. Vintage woodcraft books and magazines are full of plans and directions for shelves, some of them easy and some of them not.

The Varied Forms & Uses of Retro Craft Are Limitless

Bottlecap men have two bowls ready and waiting to serve. Keep one in your office area to catch paper clips and rubber bands. One graces my art desk, gathering marbles, beads, and other things I want to sort and put away later. (A word of caution: Bottlecap men are known pranksters, prone to tumping their lower bowls the moment you put something in them. Before you load them up, test and shore up, if necessary.)

Lamps were a favorite with retro crafters, with match-sticks, cigar boxes, and popsicle sticks well represented in the genre. A recently and properly rewired piece is a

Vintage corner shelves ranging in size from 18 to 42 inches tall

A box decoupaged with flowers clipped from greeting cards holds earrings, woodburned boxes hold their namesakes, and a box lavishly festooned with gold fringe is stylish storage for sunglasses.

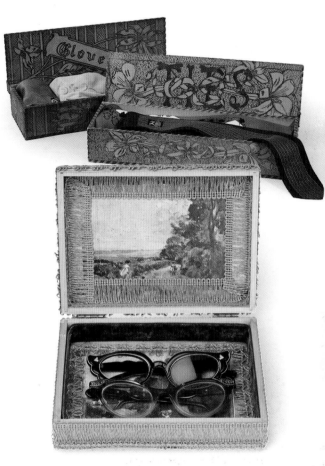

Retro craft boxes come in every size with all types of encrustation: decoupage, matchsticks, shells, macaroni, etc. Put them to work, in your home or in your office. A battalion of them hold the jewelry on my dresser top, while a smaller cluster of them in my dressing area hold hair accessories and wayward buttons.

The most effortless function for retro craft is to serve as home decor. Buy something and plunk it down somewhere—done, done, and done. The simple materials and inescapable handmadeness are homey, and often have a wink of humor. Adding a unique piece of retro craft lends originality to any decorating scheme. It's the very embodiment of "conversation piece."

Say "When"

If you lean toward the safe side, choose more subtle pieces: a small box encrusted with seashells, a notched frame, a decorated bottle. If your style is bold, choose an outrageous lamp, a pair of fabulous paint by numbers, or a large bowl made of rusted bottlecaps.

You can use a piece or two as accents, or deck the halls with true abandon. Let retro craft be the spice in your decor, and season to taste. Regardless of the motif, it can hold its own and then some.

Bless This Excess
A clunky wood-burned horse plaque holds its own in the chaos that is my kitchen pantry.

The Retro Craft Hostess

Serving with Style

Add some retro craft panache to your entertaining. Let your personal style, mood, or the occasion dictate whether you add just a few subtle inspired touches, or whether you pull out the stops.

Consider choosing a theme for your festivities. Working around a theme makes the event more memorable, and can actually make the planning easier by giving focus to your choices.

Invitations

Sending invitations is a lovely gesture. The decision to do so or not is entirely between you and Miss Manners. If you opt to send them, consider retro crafting them. They'll be appreciated for their personal touch and their quirky charm. When making invitations, crafty crafters choose a level of complexity in reverse proportion to the number of invitations they have to produce—i.e., if it's a small gathering, knock yourself out; if there are dozens and dozens to make, be realistic.

Card making is one of the most common projects found in retro craft books and periodicals. Vintage Christmas periodicals are swimming with retro-crafty card ideas. No matter that they're holiday specific— borrow design and assembly ideas from them, and replace the holiday imagery with something that relates to the occasion at hand.

Place Cards

If your soiree is a seated one, make place cards. They're both a throwback to a more genteel time, and a time-honored, megalomaniacal means of force-mingling your guests. They're a snap to make.

The fastest, easiest place card is a 3" x 3" piece of cardstock folded in half and bearing the name of the guest. If you have aspirations beyond fast and easy, add embellishments that relate to the theme or occasion. Cut out the paper in interesting shapes. Cut fun imagery from vintage magazines and glue it to the cards. Make small retro craft figures to hold them, or use vintage game pieces. (I'm getting so enthused here, I want to plan a party so I have an excuse to make them.)

Be flattered when your guests surreptitiously slip them from the table to keep as mementos.

Centerpieces and Decorations

A three-step retro craft centerpiece;

1   Start with a retro craft vase or vessel of some sort (line it with a plain glass jar if necessary)

2   Stuff flowers in it

3   Fill it with water

Now brush your hands together and go on break. If you're feeling more creative or more inspired, let that be your starting point. Add candles, retro craft figures or objects, a serving dish with greenery or fruit. Let it sprawl. Centerpieces can be elaborate, but keep them low so they don't hinder conversation.

Table spreads pictured in vintage ladies' magazines and cookbooks often feature additional decorations scattered across the serving table and throughout the house. Here's a tip from a frequently harried hostess: Focus on the focal points. Those would be near the entrance where you'll greet your guests, in the guest bathroom, and in the main area where you plan on entertaining folks. If you know that they'll all end up in the kitchen, save yourself the time and trouble and just make your extra touches in there. Inspired by an artist friend of mine who had a permanent diorama featuring models of Godzilla and vintage cars in his freezer (much to the annoyance of his ice-cream-loving roommates), I like to add a little decorative touch inside the refrigerator or freezer as an unexpected surprise. Try a coterie of happy vegetable people reclining on a plate or a little snow village. Nothing says *joie de vivre* like decorations in the icebox.

What could be more appropriate refrigerator decor, than a plump, edible penguin? This food-craft classic is made with an egg body, giant ripe olive head and wings, and bright carrot bit beak and feet. Make a mini penguin by replacing the egg body with another black olive. Hold it all together with cream cheese.

Serving Suggestions

When retro-taining, go one step beyond using vintage or vintage-looking serving pieces and include some retro craft pieces as servers. You can use actual vintage craft pieces, or retro craft pieces you have created. Of course, don't use anything that doesn't scrub up well, or that doesn't seem clean and hygienic. Always line the craft piece. Clear glass plates and bowls work great as liners with anything you serve. They show off the pieces while keeping them clean and separate from the food. Towels or napkins (cloth or paper) and paper doilies work fine for lining pieces serving dry foods.

If you've never pressed your collectibles into duty on the buffet table before, override your assumptions, and look at the craft pieces in terms of how they could work as serving pieces. Some things that easily lend themselves to serving are listed in the chart below.

Hand-built ceramics figures step down from the bookshelf from time to time to serve salt and pepper on the buffet table.

Serve with Verve

BASKETS & BOWLS

SHOPPING LISTS & WOODBURNED BOARDS

DECOUPAGED ITEMS

Fitted with linings, baskets, and bowls of all sorts, bottle-cap, Popsicle stick, twiggery, etc., are ready and at your service.

Use a wooden shopping list or woodburned board under a bowl or plate to serve as a smart trivet or serving tray.

There are a broad variety of decoupaged items available for gracing your table: plates, bowls, boxes, and more. Or make your own reverse decoupage sweet plate (page 100). One of my favorite pieces is a decoupaged canister decorated with pictures of ranch homes and cookies.

FOLDED PAPER CHAIN BOXES AND MATS

BOTTLECAP MAN

HAND-BUILT CERAMICS

Folded paper chain boxes or mats need to be well lined and, even after you line them, avoid using paper crafts to serve anything drippy, such as dip.

Although bottlecap men were made to be servers, I still line the bowls of vintage pieces with other bowls. It seems more hygienic and makes cleanup much easier.

I'm crazy for hand-built ceramic pieces, the more awkwardly rendered, the better. But don't trust the glaze of your yard sale find. It may contain lead or other toxins. Always use a liner so the food isn't touching the glaze.

Mmm-mm, Gooey!

Maybe middle America was eating meat and potatoes, but the ladies' magazines of the 1950s and '60s were touting the likes of fishstick pizza, and "penny cakes" (pancakes adorned with slices of wieners). Preparing retro recipes can be a form of retro craft. Both emphasize embellishment and presentation. Vintage recipes often call for extensive tweaking of food after it's prepared—garnishes gone wild! It's retro crafting with edible objects.

Serving retro food can be a big hoot when it's presented, but after the laughter dies down, the dish may well fall short of your usual culinary standards. Consider serving food that's retro in character and presentation, but not literally retro. Almost anything in retro serving pieces with a ridiculously over-done garnish can pass as retro food. Serve a potato salad with a bouquet of egg-slice-bloom and green-onion-stem flowers on top. Poke a pair of olive eyes, a midget carrot nose, and a pimento smile into a big bowl of macaroni and cheese. Top everything, from the salad course through dessert, with maraschino cherries. Everything.

Make these foamy friends to brighten up your bar,

cap your cupcakes, dress up a dowdy casserole, or coax a toddler to the table.

Animal Pals Party Picks

Work on a tray and prep all your materials before you begin to assemble. Start with colorful toothpicks and cocktail straws. Pick a limited palette of colors to work with; it'll make them feel more like a set. Punch or cut circles from the foam to make heads and "cowls" (these are 1⅜"). To cover the backs of their heads, punch or cut same-size circles of decorative paper. Cut egg shapes out of white paper for eyes. Hole punch tiny black circles for pupils. A standard hole punch works great for making noses out of glitter foam. Little foam bow ties have matching punched "knots." Cut tiny slivers of white paper for whiskers. I punched some circles from sandpaper just because I like the texture—they ended up inside the bear's ears. Once you have a tray brimming with possibilities—and here's your real TV chef moment—slide the tray onto your work area, sit down with a box of glue dots, and just start having fun.

Mix and match. Cut ears from the same color foam as the cowl. Sandwich the straws and toothpicks between the foam face and decorative paper with glue dots. Use a toothpick and tacky craft glue to attach paper accessories like the eyes and whiskers. Draw the mouths with a fine-point permanent marker. If you think you can't freehand the mouth, turn the critter on its side, with its ears to the left, and draw a "3" to the right of its nose. You're a pro now.

Would you trust these ladies to contribute mouth-watering baked macaroni and cheese to a potluck dinner? Of course you would! They're suited up and ready to serve.

Tying One On

An apron, that is. In general, I encourage you to choose what aspects of retro craft living you want to embrace and the degree of commitment you want to invest. On this one point, however, I'm ridiculously inflexible: You can't be a proper retro craft hostess without an apron. Period. It's like drinking moonshine from a stemmed glass, or eating spaghetti in your car—it's just not right.

For starters, vintage aprons are retro craft. Even when made from directions or patterns, most vintage aprons feature handwork and embellishment that make them distinctive. The fabrics and colors are dead-on accurate period references for any retro crafter. They're functional functionaries of the era which they were made.

Like walking in a bowling alley with your own ball and shoes, when you sweep into the kitchen in an apron, people assume you know what you're doing. It's a uniform, especially when paired with high heels. To your guests, it conveys confidence. And the pockets are a great place to hide the mini bottles.

Bread Wrapper Apron

How many times have you seen a festive, plastic bread wrapper and thought, gee, I wish I could wear that thing? Okay, maybe you haven't, but you've got to admit, there are some colorful, fun bread wrappers out there. Start with four of them, three for the apron skirt and one for the pocket.

1 Cut down the side seams and across the sealed end of the bread bags. Figure out how you want to lay out the panels.

2 Lay the center panel facedown on a clean, flat surface. (I like to work on an ironing board—it's clean, flat, and uncluttered.) Run a strip of double-sided tape down the entire length of both sides of the center panel. Carefully place the side panels facedown into the tape, and smooth out. Trim the top and bottom edges of the panels even (if necessary).

3 Cut a small piece for the pocket, about 6" x 6". Put it facedown on the work surface. Run a strip of double-sided tape about ¾" down from the top edge, running the entire width of the pocket. Fold the top edge down over the tape, and smooth it out. Still working on the back of the pocket, run strips of double-sided tape down both sides and across the bottom, very close to the edges. Turn it over, and put it in place on the apron.

4 Turn ½" of the top edge of the apron over toward the back. With needle and thread, make large basting stitches across the doubled-over top edge, leaving at least 2" of thread on both ends. Holding the threads on one end, gently pull on the other threads to evenly gather the top edge, till it's about 12" wide. Knot and tie the threads on both ends.

5 To attach a waistband, put a strip of double-sided tape all the way across the front of the top edge. Line up the center of a 2" x 20" ribbon with the center of the apron skirt and press it in place, lining up the bottom edge of the ribbon with the bottom edge of the tape.

This cheeky plastic fashion statement is fabulous for serving or crafting, but stay out of the kitchen—a warm breeze from the oven door or other source of heat could leave you melting like the wicked witch.

Retro Craft-a-Go-Go

Have you ever found yourself:

riding in the passenger seat on a long trip when nobody wants to play the alphabet game or auto bingo?

in an airport, train, or bus station, involved with any aspect of travel, either as the traveler or the waiting-for-the-traveler person?

sitting in a waiting room with nothing to read but outdated magazines of no interest to you?

You need a grab-and-go craft kit! Having a craft kit packed and ready to go can save you from many an hour of boredom.

I like to craft when I'm out of town. It amuses me because it's fun and because it's ridiculous. There are times when I bring a kit along and never open it, and other times when working on a craft project is the best part of the trip.

To put together a grab-and-go craft kit:

1 Choose a suitable project. *(See next page for suggestions.)*

2 Think through what you'll need in addition to the project supplies to make working away from home easier: *a clip-on book light for working in places with poor lighting; an extension cord; a baby food jar with water if there are brushes to clean; something to collect scraps in, if your craft generates them; and something to safely hold the finished work. I try to be totally self-contained so I don't have to rely on the kindness of strangers.*

3 Pick a styling case for packing your kit. *Make it fun: a faux alligator 8-track case, an old metal first aid kit, Grandpa's retired black lunch pail.*

4 Invest in kit-designated tools. *It negates the grab-and-go aspect if you have to pack additional things.*

5 If you're the social sort, consider packing a finished example of whatever your project is. *Crafting in unexpected places invites curiosity. Someone is going to ask what you're making, and it's fun to show off what the result will be.*

It's handy for craft kits to include a mini satellite unit that has materials and tools to make one step of a project. This decoupage kit contains a slim vinyl bag for scissors and rough-cut imagery that needs to be finely trimmed. The folded paper chain kit (next page, lower right) includes a small case with strips that are cut and ready to be folded. Either satellite unit could be tucked into a shoulder bag or pocket to be taken with you when you don't have the time or inclination to work on the full project.

Previous page:

Reverse decoupage kit

This small case packs a clown-car punch, with everything needed to make reverse decoupage plates. It includes vintage magazines and small cookbooks, paper doilies, paper towels, acrylic medium, scissors, a craft knife and spare blades, a small container of water, a foam brush, sponges, a bowl, a large plate to use as a work surface, and glass plates, protected by sheets of felt and tucked safe and snug into an old holiday tin.

Beaded whimsey kit

A thrift-store cosmetic case has all the makings for a whimsey, from start to finish, including the templates, fabric, cardboard, spray adhesive, tracing paper, beads, thread, scissors, pencil, ruler, and needles. Non-essentials that are handy to have include small cups to pour beads into, index cards with pictures of reference pieces, tiny clothespins to hold the bead pattern in place while tracing it, and a small box of assorted beads *(held closed with a pony tail holder).*

A kit for a time-consuming project such as whimsey making is ideal for an out-of-town trip, because a minimal amount of materials will keep you crafting for a very long time.

Matchstick kit

Unburned matches, loose and boxed, are packed in storage containers. Burnt matches fit perfectly in a mint tin. Additional supplies include an ashtray, tea candle, rag to wipe ashes from the matchsticks, and paper place mats to protect the work surface. Everything tucks neatly into a tin with picnic handles. Frequently, I tuck precut cardboard and a small container of white glue into my kit for making frames.

Folded paper chain kit

This kit is packed into a vinyl record tote. It includes a mini trimmer, ruler, needle, thread, nail clipper (for trimming thread), CD case full of trimmed strips, small case to hold the containers full of strips and finished paper chains, lunch bag for scraps, and a piece of foam core cut to fit the box, to use as a mini lap desk when needed.

A Retro Craft Mindset

Paper chain frame
Gum wrappers
8 x 6 inches
My mother sharing the lawn with a
flock of hand-crafted chickens

There's more to retro craft than the fun and googly-eyed appeal. Creating and collecting retro craft can be a soulful, endlessly creative connection to your roots. It's a great way to share time with family and friends since there's practically no one too young or too old to join in. I find it equally rewarding as a solitary avocation. There's a lot of time for introspection as you glue matchsticks on a pencil case.

Retro crafting encourages ingenuity. It allows you to enjoy the excitement of being creative without imposing any fun-killing expectations on the results. Savor the luxury of spending an afternoon making silly things.

Retro craft has helped me to rediscover the joy of making things just because it's fun. I sincerely hope it can do something equally meaningful for you.

Templates

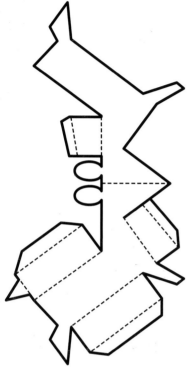

Hoppy Holiday
Reinbeer!

Page 74

Copy all templates at 200% to make the projects as shown, or any size you'd like to make them differently.

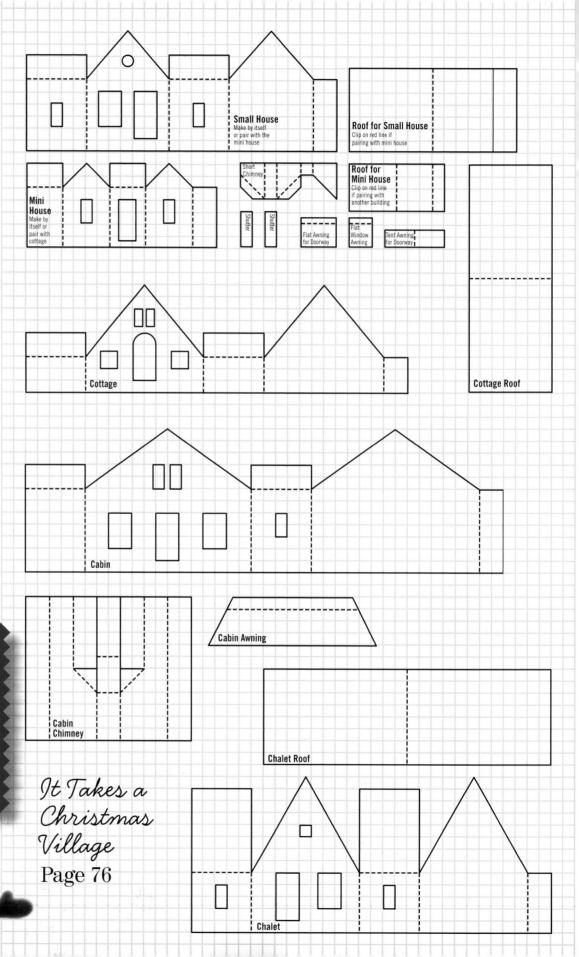

Small House
Make by itself
or pair with the
mini house

Roof for Small House
Clip on red line if
pairing with mini house

Mini House
Make by
itself or
pair with
cottage

Short Chimney

Roof for Mini House
Clip on red line
if pairing with
another building

Shutter

Shutter

Flat Awning for Doorway

Flat Window Awning

Tent Awning for Doorway

Cottage

Cottage Roof

Cabin

Cabin Awning

Cabin Chimney

Chalet Roof

It Takes a
Christmas
Village
Page 76

Chalet

Body

Pocket

Beaded
Whimsey
Pocket
Page 130

Handy Ribbon Spacer
PUT DOWN THAT HEAVY RULER AND JUST USE THIS
TO MARK WHERE TO PLACE THE DOUBLE-SIDED TAPE

For all templates:

———————— = Cut

------------ = Score

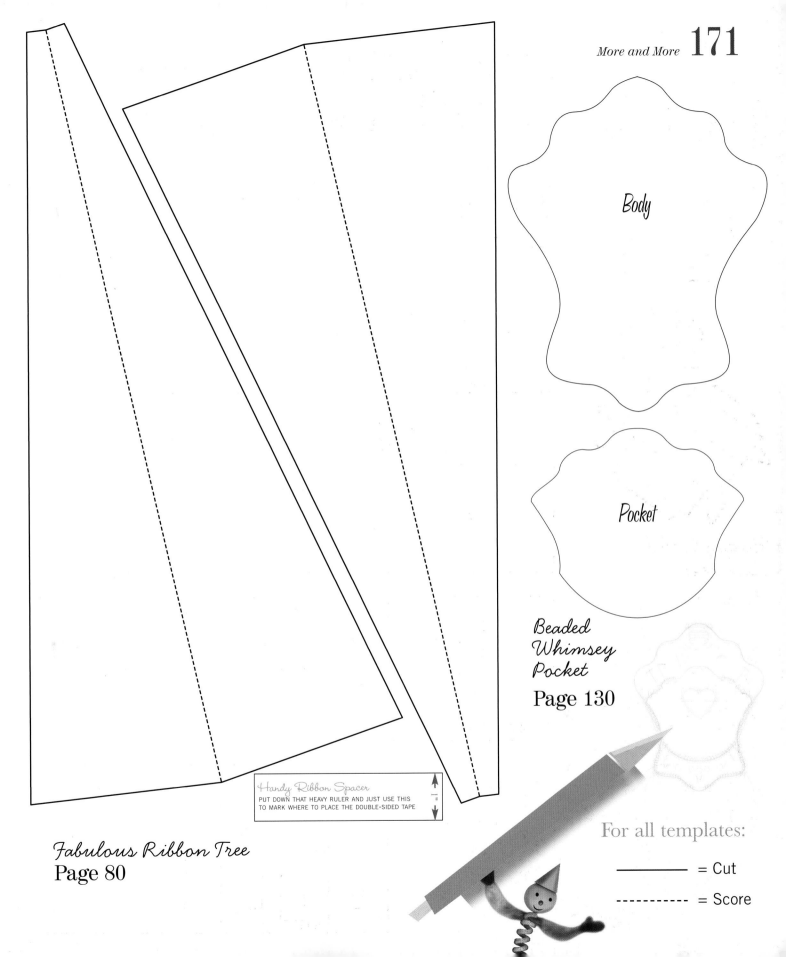

Gift Giving Ideas

Need a gift-idea-nudge for a baby shower, wedding, Father's Day, or other special event?
Check the chart.

Every project in the book is listed here. Lightly shaded boxes indicate projects that are appropriate for an occasion without alterations. The darker shaded boxes indicate projects appropriate with some alteration. Some specific ideas for alterations are listed on the next page.

Project	Page	BABY	CHILD	MANLY	HOST/ESS	ROMANTIC	YULE
Glitter Frame	P. 52						
Sparkling Sputnik	P. 54						
Ooh la la Lampshade	P. 57						
Pantyhose Poodle	P. 58						
Pillbox Party Hat	P. 60						
Glitter Critters	P. 61						
Paper Chain Frame	P. 64						
Postcard Frame	P. 66						
Basket Purse	P. 67						
Starburst Clock	P. 68						
45 rpm Record Tote	P. 70						
Reinbeer	P. 74						
Tin Can Tree	P. 75						
Christmas Village	P. 76						
Pinecone Elf	P. 79						
Ribbon Tree	P. 80						
Trinket Box	P. 85						
Split Spool Planter	P. 86						
Candy Dish	P. 87						
Haberdashery Box	P. 88						
Pleather Jar	P. 91						
Wind Chime	P. 92						
Just a Memento	P. 95						
Baby Food Jar Circus	P. 96						
Pseudo Souvenirs	P. 99						
Sweet Sweet Plate	P. 100						
Whimsey Bottle	P. 102						
Phone Pardner	P. 107						
Teacup Cuties	P. 108						
Plaster Plaques	P. 110						
Frame Tray	P. 112						
Bottle Buddies	P. 114						
Pill Bottle Shrines	P. 115						
Plastic Flower Pixies	P. 116						
Matchbook Notebook	P. 119						
Matchstick Desk Caddy	P. 120						
Matchstick Frame	P. 122						
Matchbox Drawers	P. 125						
Button Necklace	P. 127						
Garden Box	P. 128						
Whimsey Pocket	P. 130						
Wash Mitts	P. 132						
Snap Album	P. 135						
Bottlecap Man	P. 136						
Spool Shelves	P. 138						
Yardstick Organizers	P. 140						
Towel Holder	P. 141						
Animal Pals Party Picks	P. 165						
Bread Wrapper Apron	P. 166						

Baby Gift

Use pastel colors, and add a satiny ribbon whenever you can

Make the Glitter Frame, in pink, blue, or neutral yellow. Decorate the top with a plastic trinket from the baby shower aisle of your craft store. Use children's book imagery to make the Ooh La La Lampshade, Postcard Frame, Just a Memento, or Plaster Plaques. Make a decaffeinated Paper Chain Frame for the nursery using pastel paper strips. Use children's imagery to make a Frame Tray or Garden Box for the baby's dresser top. As pictured, make the Bundle of Joy variation of the Plastic Flower Pixie, or a Jar Circus.

Child's Gift

Use imagery from comic books, children's picture books, children's encyclopedias, or text books.

There are some kids that will enjoy the projects without any alteration needed. The Pantyhose Poodle directions can be altered to make other critters (drop the cheeky cigarette, *s'il vous plaît*). The Christmas Village has a kids' gift box variation (page 77). Cover the Matchstick Desk Caddy with children's imagery instead of matches. Decorate the Matchbox Drawers with toys and trinkets and fill with toys or colored pencils and other art supplies. Make the Yardstick Organizer using picture book covers instead of yardsticks. Jar Circus animals loaded up with treats make great party favors.

Host/ess Gift

Many of the projects in the book could be suitable as a host/ess gift. My favorite host gift is a Teacup Cutie bearing a live herb. A close second, a Bottle Buddy topping a kitchen product. During the holidays, any of the Crazy for Christmas projects would make a lovely gift for the host.

Manly Gift

Cars, fish, and pin-up girls are generally accepted manly imagery. All manner of matchstick decor is a-ok.

Like the unique children that will enjoy a retro craft gift without any special alteration, there are plenty of guys that would enjoy almost any of the projects here made as directed. There are other men that would perhaps enjoy some of the projects more if they were made with some he-manly adjustments—no glitter or pantyhose poofs, please. Make a Memento with a photo from a favorite fishing trip, decorated with a feathery fly lure or pine cones instead of a bow; use an old plate from a camping kit. Make an whip-stitched box with pages from automotive or girlie magazines, instead of seed packets.

Romantic Gift

For weddings, bridal showers, and other nuptial events, alter projects using flowers, doves, joined rings, and lots of white (or specific bridal theme colors if you know them.)

The Glitter Frame and Paper Chain Frame can be made with bridal or Valentine colors. Alter the Horseshoe variation of the glitter frame to be a heart. Make the Postcard Frame using romantic turn-of-the-century postcards. Pillbox Hats decorated with bridal wrapping paper and dove tipped antennae would dress up any bridal shower. For the less ambitious, just make one for the bride-to-be. In my house, nothing could be more romantic than a hand-made 45rpm Record Tote. The one pictured on page 70 with vintage girlie imagery was a Valentine gift to my sweetheart. A Sweet Sweet Plate is a wonderful wedding gift. Filled with cookies, it's a Valentine to remember.

Yule

Almost any project in this book can be made holiday-friendly by adding a bit of plastic holly and some spray snow. Make a Holiday Party Hat with old Christmas gift wrap. Use Christmas record album covers and old holiday greeting cards as imagery, cardstock, or cardstock with imagery (for a Paper Chain Frame, Plaster Plaque, or Glitter Frame). Instead of a Pantyhose Poodle, make a sleigh team of wobbly holiday reindeer. Make a baby food jar nativity, or Teacup Cutie rimmed with tinsel and filled with Christmas greens.

Metric Conversion Chart

INCHES	METRIC (MM/CM)	INCHES	METRIC (MM/CM)	INCHES	METRIC (MM/CM)	INCHES	METRIC (MM/CM)	INCHES	METRIC (MM/CM)	INCHES	METRIC (MM/CM)
1/4	6 mm	1	2.5 cm	8 1/2	21.6 cm	16 1/2	41.9 cm	24 1/2	62.2 cm	32 1/2	82.6 cm
1/8	3 mm	1 1/2	3.8 cm	9	22.9 cm	17	43.2 cm	25	63.5 cm	33	83.8 cm
3/16	5 mm	2	5 cm	9 1/2	24.1 cm	17 1/2	44.5 cm	25 1/2	64.8 cm	33 1/2	85 cm
1/4	6 mm	2 1/2	6.4 cm	10	25.4 cm	18	45.7 cm	26	66 cm	34	86.4 cm
5/16	8 mm	3	7.6 cm	10 1/2	26.7 cm	18 1/2	47 cm	26 1/2	67.3 cm	34 1/2	87.6 cm
3/8	9.5 mm	3 1/2	8.9 cm	11	27.9 cm	19	48.3 cm	27	68.6 cm	35	88.9 cm
7/16	1.1 cm	4	10.2 cm	11 1/2	29.2 cm	19 1/2	49.5 cm	27 1/2	69.9 cm	35 1/2	90.2 cm
1/2	1.3 cm	4 1/2	11.4 cm	12	30.5 cm	20	50.8 cm	28	71.1 cm	36	91.4 cm
9/16	1.4 cm	5	12.7 cm	12 1/2	31.8 cm	20 1/2	52 cm	28 1/2	72.4 cm	36 1/2	92.7 cm
5/8	1.6 cm	5 1/2	14 cm	13	33 cm	21	53.3	29	73.7 cm	37	94.0 cm
11/16	1.7 cm	6	15.2 cm	13 1/2	34.3 cm	21 1/2	54.6	29 1/2	74.9 cm	37 1/2	95.3 cm
3/4	1.9 cm	6 1/2	16.5 cm	14	35.6 cm	22	55 cm	30	76.2 cm	38	96.5 cm
13/16	2.1 cm	7	17.8 cm	14 1/2	36.8 cm	22 1/2	57.2 cm	30 1/2	77.5 cm		
7/8	2.2 cm	7 1/2	19 cm	15	38.1 cm	23	58.4 cm	31	78.7 cm		
15/16	2.4 cm	8	20.3 cm	15 1/2	39.4 cm	23 1/2	59.7 cm	31 1/2	80 cm		
				16	40.6 cm	24	61 cm	32	81.3 cm		

Special Thanks

I owe an awful lot of thanks to people who've helped to make this book. First, to my husband Lance, for his professional support as the production coordinator, and for his personal support and patience. Our home and studio were in a state of retro craft chaos for well over a year and he never complained.

To Megan Kirby, for approaching me with the idea for the book, and all the encouragement she gave along the way.

At Lark Books, my editor Ronni Lundy and editor-in-chief Deborah Morgenthal went above and beyond the call of duty keeping the project moving. When presented with a long list that resembled a ludicrous scavenger hunt, Susan Kieffer worked extra hard securing copyright clearances. Art director Chris Bryant gave me the opportunity to be my own art director, and provided me with the training wheels I needed as I wobbled along.

Special thanks to William Swislow for graciously welcoming Lance and me into his home to see and photograph his collection, and for sharing his own photographs of the *Outside the Lines* show at Intuit. Folk art collector Alan Phillips also generously opened his home and alerted me to Susan Jones's definitive book, *Genius in a Bottle*. Red Heel Monkey Shelter owners Letitia Walker and Whitney Shroyer gave time and encouragement.

With deadlines looming, I had help making my projects. Master sputnik maker Jennifer Jessee assembled the sputnik and the coffee loving Record Tote. She decorated the Horseshoe Frame, Treasured Treasure Box, and the precious Children's Gift Box. She also helped me finish my Beaded Whimsey Pocket. My massively creative friend Charmayne taught me how to make the party hat, and models one she made on page 50. The Christmas Village and teacup cuties were a combined effort of the Blue Ridge Craft Clatch—Sharon Belcher, Esther Cartwright, Shannon George, Jennifer Jessee, Christi Whiteley, and myself. Christi Whitely stitched the Chirpy and Foxy bath mitts. I designed and decorated Snappy Cappy and the towel holder, both were put together by Jamie Stirling. Very special thanks to artist and all around creative person Jim Lindsey, who taught me how to make the button necklaces, and made the examples used in this book.

Special thanks to my father for teaching me how to be practical and analytical, and to my mother, for giving me permission to selectively ignore that advice from time to time.

Last, but so far from least, big thank yous to my good friends and artistic collaborators, Marisol Hernandez in New Orleans, and Lee Swets in Memphis, for all the inspiration, kindness, and encouragement they've provided through the years, and to all the other friends, family, collectors, and gallery owners who've helped me keep my head above the storm surge.

Credits

Cover

Cover artwork © Juli Waller, Grrraphics

Page 5

Photo of Lance and Suzie, courtesy and © Theresa Kereakes

Page 12

Tramp art box, courtesy William Swislow, photo Lance Wille

Sock monkey, Spark Plug, courtesy Whitney Shroyer and Letitia Walker, Red Heel Monkey Shelter

Cigarette package folded chain frame, courtesy Jennifer Jessee

Bottlecap toy chair, courtesy William Swislow, photo Lance Wille

Page 13

Boys and girls crafting, 1951, photo courtesy of the Lindley G. Cook 4-H Youth Center for Outdoor Education, Branchville, New Jersey

Page 14

Flip toy, courtesy William Swislow, photo Lance Wille

Michigan State Prison, Marquette, Michigan, photo courtesy of Michigan State Prison

Page 16—All photos courtesy and © William Swislow

Images of Banner, Sphinx, & Lamp can be found at:

http://www.interestingideas.com/ii/files

WWI Victory Banner, ca. 1914-15, courtesy of Carl Hammer Gallery, Chicago, Illinois

Tom Cartwright, Untitled (Great Sphinx), ca. 1945-1950, courtesy the Collection of John Cain

Page 17

Popsicle-Stick Lamp, courtesy the collection of Reid Brody, photo courtesy and © William Swislow

List of 80 craft items used in illustration, from the article "The Art of Popular Craft" by William Swislow, Volume 8, Issue 3, Spring 2004, pages 21-29, reprinted, by permission, from *Outsider* magazine

Page 18

Vintage trailer, photo courtesy Joni and Greg Neutra

Page 31

Hernando's Hide-A-Way matchbook, courtesy of Hernando's Hide-A-Way, Memphis, Tennessee

Page 40

Vintage clothespins, courtesy of Erin Roth, the ScreenDoor, Asheville, North Carolina

Page 41

Vintage bracelet, courtesy of Corinne Kurzman, Diggin' Art, Asheville, North Carolina

Page 50

Glittered shrine, courtesy of William Swislow, photo Lance Wille

Page 52

Horseshoe frame, courtesy of Erin Roth, the ScreenDoor, Asheville, North Carolina

Page 56

Joe's Liquor, photo courtesy Lee Swets

Page 62

Matchbook frame, Dick Dehner, Untitled, 1938, 30 x 30 x 11½ inches, photo © Cheri Eisenberg, courtesy the private collection of Cheri Eisenberg

Folded paper chain chair, courtesy of William Swislow, photo Lance Wille

Page 63

Double cigarette wrapper folded chain frame, courtesy Eldorado Modern, Asheville, North Carolina

Cigarette wrapper folded chain frame, courtesy Jennifer Jessee

Page 69

Wall clocks, *Sears 1961 Spring-Summer Catalog*, Page 1246, image courtesy of Sears Brands, LLC

Page 72 and 73

Holiday figures and pinecone people, courtesy of Eldorado Modern, Asheville, North Carolina

Christmas village, courtesy of Magnolia Beauregard's Antiques, Asheville, North Carolina

Page 74

Alcoa ad featuring Kenny Rogers, courtesy Alcoa and Kenny Rogers

Page 78

Country Christmas, Loretta Lynn, 1980, MCA Records, MCA-5022, courtesy Universal Music Group

For a Musical Merry Christmas, Vol. 4, Special Collectors Edition, RCA Victor Stereo PRS-253, © 1967, RCA album artwork courtesy of SONY BMG Entertainment

Page 82

Round encrusted box, courtesy of little Miss Ivy

Page 84

Macaroni tree illustration by Jennifer Jessee

Page 118

Matchstick frame, courtesy of Simon and Christi Whiteley

Page 126

Sweetheart Doll: The Majorette, No. s173, Series 2, Vintage Crochet Sheet, The Spool Cotton Company, © 1951 Coats & Clark Inc, reproduced with permission of Coats & Clark Inc.

Vintage beaded whimsey, courtesy of Linda Dean

Crocheted pot holders, courtesy of Jennifer Jessee

Stitch chart, excerpted from *Handicrafts and Hobbies*, © 1948. Published by Greystone Press. Reprinted with permission from Meredith Corporation.

Page 134

Line-up of bottlecap men, photos courtesy of William Swislow, photos © William Swislow

Page 145

Burl Room, vintage postcard from the *Big Trees of Santa Cruz County* album, Vester Dick. Published by Donmar Sales Co, Santa Cruz, CA. Photograph used with permission from Covello & Covello Photography, Santa Cruz, CA

Page 148

Learn How Book, Spool Cotton Co. book #170-A, © 1952 Coats & Clark Inc., Reproduced with permission of Coats & Clark Inc.

Star Pot Holders, American Thread Co. book #32, © Coats & Clark Inc., Reproduced with permission of Coats & Clark Inc.

Page 162

Table setting illustration by Jennifer Jessee

Page 166

1965 Chrysler Newport, courtesy of Kip Veno

Index